Also by Brenda Hillman

POETRY

White Dress

Fortress

Death Tractates

Bright Existence

Loose Sugar

Cascadia

Pieces of Air in the Epic

Practical Water

Seasonal Works with Letters on Fire

Extra Hidden Life, among the Days

CHAPBOOKS

Coffee, 3 A.M.

Autumn Sojourn

The Firecage

Four Poets (with Brett Fletcher Lauer, Joshua Marie Wilkinson, and
 Andrew Zawacki)

Her Presence Will Live Beyond Progress

AS EDITOR

The Poems of Emily Dickinson

The Grand Permission: New Writings on Poetics and Motherhood
 (with Patricia Dienstfrey)

Writing the Silences: Selected Poems of Richard O. Moore (with Paul Ebenkamp)

Particulars of Place by Richard O. Moore (with Garrett Caples and Paul Ebenkamp)

AS TRANSLATOR

Instances by Jeonrye Choi (with the author and Wayne de Fremery)

Poems from Above the Hill: Selected Poems of Ashur Etwebi (with the author and Diallah Haidar)

At Your Feet by Ana Cristina Cesar (with Helen Hillman and Sebastião Macedo)

In a
Few
Minutes
Before
Later

Brenda Hillman

Wesleyan
University
Press

Middletown, Connecticut

In a
Few
Minutes
Before
Later

Wesleyan Poetry

Wesleyan University Press

Middletown CT 06459

www.wesleyan.edu/wespress

© 2022 Brenda Hillman

All rights reserved

Manufactured in the United States of America

First paperback edition 2024

Paperback ISBN 978-0-8195-0122-6

Designed and composed by Crisis

Library of Congress Cataloging-in-Publication Data

Names: Hillman, Brenda, author.

Title: In a few minutes before later / Brenda Hillman.

Description: Middletown, Connecticut : Wesleyan University Press, [2022] |
    Series: Wesleyan poetry | Summary: "Poems meditating on differences
    between human time and ecological time, bringing to the foreground
    experiences of love and aging"—Provided by publisher.

Identifiers: LCCN 2022024357 (print) | LCCN 2022024358 (ebook) |
    ISBN 9780819500151 (cloth) | ISBN 9780819500229 (ebook)

Subjects: BISAC: POETRY / Subjects & Themes / Nature | POETRY /
    Subjects & Themes / Family | LCGFT: Poetry.

Classification: LCC PS3558.I4526 I5 2022 (print) | LCC PS3558.I4526 (ebook) |
    DDC 811/.54—dc23

LC record available at https://lccn.loc.gov/2022024357

LC ebook record available at https://lccn.loc.gov/2022024358

5 4 3 2 1

(dedication)

These poems were composed between 2016 & 2021, half before & half during the pandemic. They were composed

- for life beside & inside the humans, non-humans, plants & kingdoms that are not plants or animals, including cyanobacteria & protozoa;
- for pre-life spirits (even if they are metaphors) seeking science threads when they arrive;
- for artists from different spiritual densities, designations, identities, & regions;
- for workers & loved ones who deliver food & flowers;
- for everyone's children & grandchildren, for Amelie, Bari, Bear, Callie, Cole, Ella, Elliott, Emily, Finn, Fiona, Gabriel, Grace, Hazel, Josephine, Leon, Lily, Malachai, Noah, Ruth, Simon, Simon, Truman & Zach;
- for 49 people who helped & forgave; for the ones we tried to forgive but cannot;
- for families who had babies during the pandemic; for Louisa, for Leah;
- for medical staff & essential medical workers; for Dr. Anthony Fauci;
- for those who endured violence & racist systems & those who protested;
- for older women, especially my mother Helen who is alive & her sister Thelma the pianist who died during the pandemic; for women & women-identified poets of all ages;
- for my brothers, making music, doing research, taking care of elders, cooking, reading the *New York Times* online & in the print edition;
- for Forrest Gander & Karin Gander;
- for creatures that kept us company indoors, for spiders that lowered themselves into bathtubs;
- for the wood rat, the fox & coyote, for two squirrels that learned to operate the squirrel-proof birdfeeder till the spring broke, for the fawn that ate the baby lettuces while its mother watched, for powdery mildew that dominated the kale & fruit flies that couldn't;
- for punctuation, especially commas & semicolons;
- for our imitators who have forgotten they imitate us;

- for the numbers 3, 6, 12, 18 & 24, & the spaces between numbers, for the between 2,103,840 & 2,628,000 minutes that passed in the making of this book;
- for the irrational growth of stressed oaks & laurels chased by Apollo; for the white moths & cabbage butterflies;
- for the great dead in dry hills praying for rain;
- for shared & unshared myths, for science & magic in equal parts;
- for the number 9 mechanical-pencil collection at Payn's Stationery Shop on Solano Avenue & for the owners, thank you for keeping a mask policy, yours is my favorite store;
- for unchartered laws of rivers & fires, for molecules of William Blake's breath;
- for Bob whose company made life matter in space & time;
- & for poetry daughters & sons who may not have time to read; this book is for you whenever you get to it, if you do at all

Contents

III. There Are Many Women to Cherish

IV. For Writers Who Are Having Trouble

V. The Sickness & the World Soul

VI. In a Few Minutes Before Later

I. Some Landscapes of Stress & Beauty

12 poems & 1 interruption

Every duration is thick; real time has no instants.
Henri Bergson, "Concerning the Nature of Time"

We lived for some years through magical thinking
G. E. Patterson, "A Linguistic Atlas of Various Worlds"

Oh, time—so long & so ago—
Lisa Alvarez

Micro-minutes on
Your Way to Work

Days are unusual. The owl sends
　　out 5 zeroes from the pines
　　　　plus one small silver nothing. Where
　　　　　　do they float? Maybe out to
　　sea, where jellyfish are aging left
& right. They have some nerve.
　　Today, no new wars, probably. No
big button. The owl could be
　　　　your scholar of trapped light or
Walter Benjamin who writes *a storm
blows in from paradise.* Thinking through
　　these things each week, you cross

the bridge: gold coils, fog, feelings . . .
　　syllables also can grow younger like
　those jellyfish. You bring your quilt
　　　　of questions in the car. At
work, you'll have to be patient
　　in the risky enterprise of talking
to other people; so little progress
　　in this since the Pleistocene. Mostly,
though, you're calm when traveling: silver
nothing, moving right & left; day
　　releasing the caged stars; one thought
mixed with no-thought, packed with light . . .

for MK

A Slightly Less Stressful Walk Uphill

How do you hope to survive?
& not just that: was it even the question?

By midday the fog was burning off;;

screech & call beside the anyway::: :::   the parent osprey
            had gone out   looking for the right fish

(did it fear stone?)   & bryophytes rested on the soil

as the soul might rest on the *what ifs*—;

you were trying not to waste poetry's time on stupid questions,

all the you's going along out there   tired,
            getting through meetings—

                never enough sleep even if you nap at the office—
                checking the phone   tiny electrons of joy,

messages from large specific you, small specific you,,
                large general you,

                pressure-filled colleagues

whose healing had not occurred   but still might . . .

Tech certainly hadn't helped; chlorpyrifos;;—
cities eking out funds, people sleeping in tents

with black & white dogs & children;

racist prisons—you're getting numb to the list—"growth
in the service sector"—

women working three jobs—production of power

& that tone in the profit voices when you call customer service
growing slightly more officious suspecting the next "downturn"—

you wake with nano-minutes of stress built up overnight—
    offshore breezes,   fear of fires—

mosses bunched , , , ,,, , , , ,,, , near the small oaks (did they fear stone?)

Women had experimented for centuries with too much cortisol—
so, what to do now, since doing was the problem—   It was just

mainly important to get through the day

with the minutes moving roundly, rather than lengthwise—

Surely one note could be singled out

—for example ::: ::: the screech of the baby osprey,
& the nest waiting,   heavy with proudlings—;

perhaps a calm could be entered   (like cooked fog

or a monarch butterfly coming through looking like John Clare
flying across the enclosures—)

,,, on the other side of the highway steel tubes of dairy trucks
were grinding along—

the milk sloshing inside
& besides that   the hope of

the circular spirits bringing a map of formless order

where a legendary love was taking place, beyond control—

Dawn Tercets, with Blake & Nuthatch

     & a new thought waited in its
   triangle—refusal, hope & dream— then, as you slept—light
between the commas of dawn birds (not even sure

    if the bird you hadn't seen—white-breasted nuthatch,,
could find its commas, in the tree) then:
the knowledge of *the them* you feared failing, not the test from some

thug inner government — or someone else's conscience—
 but yourself, at your most secret public,
   since language is a living thing, vital, vast — . . .

         The naturalist had
taken a knife from the group
     to slice open

an insect gall at the edge of the leaf . . . it looked like a pouty
    red lip   or a valentine. He wanted to see the larva
         inside, was slicing

to show, well, maybe
the opposite of Blake. Rose, thou art
   not exactly sick, thou art merely inhabited . . .

The instrument of change would chew itself out,
eventually. But you were human.
You wanted to be desired. Thought of.

Right Before Dusk, Some Meadow Fragments

—& there was a feeling
right before
the feeling,   sort of a pre-feeling when

it announced itself in overlapping contours
or the edges & quantity became

discernible, thing-like.   (Dread can have

a little fringe
of whiteness but
the pre-
dread has a roaming subcolor
that can go toward joy plus a soft gray pleasure
& the remaining context)—

Suppose you're in a meadow
& someone has hurt your heart;
you check your phone.

Held on the leash of now,

the moon rises.   A group
of starlings had lifted its (their?) imported heads . . .
the call was gold,

thin as a lost key,   then

yip yip yip   [*yip yip*]

                              the coyote pack, east of here.
If meaning had wings it would long have flown.

Yet experience had gathered itself, dark-eyed;
          & an odd love
                    came into focus like remaining

snow, mirroring something inexactly—

A Goodness That Comes from Nothing

Skinny afternoon moonrise,

—the stab of it, dropped

parenthesis blanched, stolen from an

earlier whiteness, & its tip   snagging the peak . . .

you walked along   (the words of your friend   having stung

from the smart phone.   What's so smart about it?)

& in the eaves of the mostly

white people hotel: mud nests   of swallows, then the word

middens came. Middens of comfort. Swallows' nests are like

anaphora in a poem, all lined up with no grief. Nothing

had been wronged there;   & around

each nest, tiny mozart flies,   keeping the tempo . . .

—golden calls from within—(some birds just sound squeezed,

particularly the babies, though

nothing has been wronged . . .)

Which voice is here, which you is living

you? It's so completely not interested in letting

go of anything.   On the mountain, marmots

would be scampering around not judged but filled snow lakes.

Sky with grisaille—an art term!—   plus gray

hatching strokes.   Though you could not be

at peace quite yet—   for now, a bristly,

stretched, signifying moon—
sometimes a song of abstract stresses leading nowhere
sometimes between each stress a helpful nothing
sometimes a goodness leading nowhere someone sees

The Highest Part of the Dust

Italic Z of snow. A perhaps raptor's nest
   beside it in the pine. Families are going in
at dusk, voices fading like numbers
   on used tram tickets run over
in the parking lot. Small bag of
dog shit placed beside a rusty pole.
Sometimes even outdoors there's a stress
you can't get out of, spinning aimlessly:

   you pass the mosses, life lifted from a rock.
Half a billion years here now—*operculum*,
   seti—the parts heaped up
without aura. Across the meadow,
   the mostly white people micro-doom
condos trying to blend in, dark glass.
   There's a specificity most things would like
to have, purpose & meaning, or:

no purpose but some meaning. You think
of the lines about the highest part
   of the dust, humans coming from that.
Mosses cling to their miracle. A blackbird
   flies through minutes all at once,
struggle & beauty in no particular
   order & you make a little doorway
in the air for that. (Or, half of a doorway . . .)

Poem Before the Power Went Out

The future was handsome before the power went out

She wrote to say he was being nice

Scythes of eucalyptus   weekday resentment
Pink Kleenex   snagged in the fence

Where did it come from   our hydropower
& if from the mountains   as if

Wind in the country   spiky sports hair
Elections   electrons   in free fall

They never knew where their power came from

Nuthatch left stripes   when it flew off

Laws paused   evening impeached them
Morning chill   of being a self

Ceasefire on rural roads   local displacement
& if from the rivers   as if

She wrote in a notebook   *Once you were calm*
Vorisively   she made up a word

Coyote bushes   filled with dire minutes
A spark whispered   not this again

Old souls   leaving the city

She called to ask   are you being strong

How can we live now   vision & science
In love with forever   stones limped along

Poem While the Power Was Out

Hot winds settled east of here;
the blurred silences began. Stripes of
the nuthatch stayed when the nuthatch
  flew off; & though you felt
the sunlight might bring harm,
  an odd forgiveness entered the suburbs
      where, like the dog in childhood,
you drew comfort from the floor.

The adults seemed baffled, wondering what
    to do next. Shouldn't they know?
 You sat quite still, & still
    all the way up your spine
reason had hung its unreasonable lights.
    O.K., then: you were supposed
  to remain strong; you knew this.
You were supposed not to worry.

Once you *were* strong; the rare
historical voices moved aside so you
  could be different. Now, afternoon was
     dark, so how to tell which
ones were real? They pressed along
through massive centuries. *What do you*
    need? What shall we do now,
they kept asking you, their ideal.

& After the Power Came Back

The great dead circled the serrated
hills; they tried to remind you
    to breathe. An old rat crawled
under fire-forgotten rocks; it was called
      & pulled to a movable nothing
    far from the human need to
      heed & heal. Maybe you can't
find it now, but the season
    hauls the wind inside & because
    you're a student you can put
some questions in your phone, especially
  when you feel you shouldn't cry . . .

Stipple the worry, the grief-torn, those
  patterns of *should* & *won't* ::; new
minutes set in past danger—spikelet
or callus on the roadside; you
    stop in awe & are home.
Your human burden varies; the once
boundless freedom you sought even in
    private still pulses on your skin . . .
    The little thistles between the human
& non-human animals, the linked auras
in trees & a colorful radiance
  of bodies are hunched to begin—

for the students

[interruption stichomythia]

—the topic of "time" has mostly been addressed in poetry

—*a timeless topic, but, yes*

—she's got a kind of batty sense of time

—*let's not malign bats iambically*

—her brain is like a hive of sleepless bees

—*that also scans*

People's Emotions in One City Block

half-shame, mild joy at hope for food, gray fear of

the walk-through monument, partial love of some humans,

cold resentment at bank options, extra pride at skin color, delight

at witnessing the number heap, shame times dread needing help,

2 quasi-firm hesitations, disgust at fried eagle, half-joy

at pride after sex, deep grief plus middle deep grief, twice

terror at law enforcement, half-worry for someone not the right one,

mild anxiety about pigeons, light interest in flower salads, oblivion

about skin color, eager reckoning at the gallery, mysterious relief

about 3s, white numbness at doorway sleepers, swell of allowable rage

craving for flower salads, semi-pride after sex, love of fire enforcement

blue terror at the bank options, craving for fried eagle, post-fear

of the number heap, furious regret at auto-correct, sweetness

of the drug in the dream, pure love of the right one, rage

at the change of schedule, dark love of hope for sex, shallow wit

plus shame, dark love of trees & birds, fear of minutes, regard for

spines & thumbs, relief for the sick one, hesitant fear before joy

for MR, Washington Square Park

After a Pageant, Before a Birth

In winter, among laws of probability
    the quiet ones merge
into earth. They sort the fertile chaos
    from flat statement.
What they derived was vital & vast,
a justice outside our usual music.
      Packed into again dry ground
         the eye-
           shaped seeds point south :::
sprout, yonderlings! We've been in touch
    with the king of thieves
        who keeps our health; all
        the wild noons hang down.

i sort the troubled jewels of intention,
i count the half-rings of the owl,
i ponder my petty resentments
    & can maybe keep
      two of the twenty-four (ponder
yonder ponder yonder); weak one,
      don't pretend you've seen enough
      to change the ratio—

      (then a whatness
seeped from the lining of our hearts,
& let us switch tones to survive—)

for BL

Poem Describing Time to the Unborn

Today the half-moon presses an obvious
ear to the sky; some clouds
   cover the alarming part. It's going
     to be a hopeful day. You,
       listening from the other side, have
not experienced sequences or fear. A
worm, crossing the battlefield, its mouth
filled with silt, will slowly become
   a blue moth while grasses spring
upward, escaping the doomed canopies. So
   the future grows at different rates.
       We think of you, inching along,

making matter, bone & blood, before
       meaning sets in. Meaning is made
of time;—oh—; winged history advances,
   the shoe is invented, the hand-held
       phone. . . . Your ancestors wove a fine
gray cloth for strangers; your parents
   have woven a name full of
     vowels to be opened when you
appear. Most minutes aren't clear. Some
   will seem tangled when they are
   lacing your shoe, but minutes will
       be better when you are here—

for MZO & EME

II. Activism & Poetry—Some Brief Reports

12 poems & 2 interruptions

for **Muriel Rukeyser, Robin Wall Kimmerer, Claudia Rankine, Rebecca Solnit, Shanee Stepakoff, Brenda Iijima, Greta Thunberg**

What does it mean to thrive?
   Lyrae Van Clief-Stefanon, from "Blooming"

It isn't that one brings life together–it's that one will not allow it to be torn apart.
   Muriel Rukeyser, from an interview, 1972

Certain effects
Would seem all at once like glamour, oracle and rubble . . .
   Eric Falci, from "Index"

The Times We Find Ourselves In

Laws were not working   so we went outside

after the shootings   the latest shootings

Mountain creek   full of summer runoff
2 centuries after Whitman's birth

The bullshit Congress   not in session   (That is so
        not respectful brenda)

Aspen & madia roots   veritable congresses
Ridged halted radials   light dragged the minutes down

Couldn't not think of the shooter's mother

Couldn't not think of dead children's hair

Couldn't not think of the gun at the gun show

But actually Walt we did not suffer   we were not there

The problem   with walking outdoors in America
Besides some yous may   be shot at any time

So little holds the ground together   It's very crumbly right now

Mountain mosses hold it   lengthwise & clockwise
Colors albeit stressed   as we are

Saw reddish ones   granitic   apex & dry-shoot

& over them extremely fluttering   migrating tortoiseshells
Ovate vacant spots   resisting their flight

Spoke of great beings   not listed in the guidebook
Their making might go on somehow

A law of misty   rootless process

A kind of light that comes from below

Activism & Poetry—A Brief Report : :: :: :

Sometimes i'm called an "activist-poet," maybe to make my aesthetically odd poetry seem more relevant or marketable to audiences other than poets. i've gotten to dislike the term "activist-poet" especially the hyphen. Mostly i'm not active & feel passive dread, bringing pagan practices outside, talking to insects & plants during the minutes etc. My practicism occurs too rarely, but basically i can't stand 95% of what is going on about anything.

On Friday of National Pollinators Week, it is suggested that we take letters to our local Kroger Market for a campaign against pesticides. Kroger uses deadly pesticides in their brand. Had signed up to drop off a letter to the manager of Kroger. i've never heard of Kroger before this; i'm from Berkeley. i drive to the nearest Kroger; my friend Jane comes along for support: she is a great calm beautiful woman. The area around the store is being gentrified & is getting whiter. We're supposed to hand letters to the managers directly.

A large percent of insect species

Will go extinct by the end of the century. i'd like to become a bee when i'm nonhuman ("b will be a bee"). My letter says Kroger's brand contains glyphosates, organophosphates & neonicotinoids. i go into the market; the security guard looks bored but the energy over her is silver. She has long brush-like eyelashes, even maybe an inch long. She points to the cashier. Endangered things in Kroger on the shelves include

Apples, sardines, plastic purple beach balls. The humans are in danger. There is Roundup. It is National Pollinator Week. The cashier calls the manager for me. He comes out. i am the only white person in Kroger. i feel shame for having come here. White person from Berkeley telling N, a worker of color not in my neighborhood, what he shouldn't have on his shelves because the bees are dying. Profit systems are full of

Violence, is my usual line . . . . . .

N, the manager, is friendly & not tired. i experience the energy over him as vital golden flecks
of winged things that could enter his circle without danger. i am a teacher, i explain; i want
humans to go on living. Can't Kroger do something i say & hand him the letter. He looks
at me with mild pity. Energy wings ^^>>< while we are talking. They never listen to us,
he says. He says, Call national Kroger

& tell them what you told me. i start to say, Kroger is committing economic terror on the peo-
ple of your city. The cereal & even the beans have been horribly sprayed. Buzzing of moral
confusion, i am a white person coming into a store not in my town to hand the letter. The
young cashier waits while this is happening, all this. She is as patient as Mary in a painting.
i say to N, can you just take my letter? He takes it. Both

Of us know they never listen to us.

To learn more about this, visit BeeAction.org, is what my letter says. Capitalism will last longer than
the bees; i saw a dead bee near our hive. Sometimes i feel terrible after "activism" but
sometimes not, depends on what gets folded in. Whether or not i feel terrible is irrelevant
but folding in the *Why feeling even a tiny bit less terrible* seems to be part of it.

for JM

In the Gardens of José Martí

You came from the shadows
with your recent friends;
at midday a mild joy entered,
then the rind

of hope; imperial history
& colonial rage
stopped at the blue door
& waited;

but a poet is like a tiny
starving cat
eating stolen food
from the fingers of the group.

When the garden sighed
in Tuesday heat, revolutionary
love was given back—past
civil law,,,, curled

in limestone walls
where workers sang
laments. What

keeps you hiding
gives you energy:
alphabet of
zeroes, cave refrains, dreams
of the little dire fishes—

for CK & SR, remembering Havana

Notes Outside West County Detention Center

The collective body sends out magnetized
        curved energy to the west,   it snags in the teeth
of the field daisies & on the hemlock
           Socrates maybe ate,
      it circles to where some stand in useless protest
under windows where the immigrants are locked

      & can't hear.   Grinding smoke from
  the refineries.
             On Fridays gray is slower.
The actions rule out rest, money for jobs or being dead
& there is mostly little news of danger here.
A white moth

drops to the asphalt, carries the suffering on two
      of its gray
      specks. No sign of life from the jail.
      There is some dust among us from before
  the sun was made, it fell in great slashes

seen by first peoples here, we place these slashes
on the instrument of time/ / /   The sheriff's men were
      later immigrants, they touch their stupid guns,
         they become magnetized
with their elbows in 7s. Some hate their jobs, some like
  policing for the state.   If love were kept

from hurt it might bend metal. The families
    stand under   the overhang while the perhaps

200 are inside for something like a traffic ticket.
ICE gave the Sheriff money for each prisoner. The Sheriff ends the contract.
Why does he end the contract? He says, & these are his exact words,
   The protests have become expensive for the county

& though i don't believe
  in hell i have placed the Sheriff's non-remorseful
soul among non-souls, a living stone with the wrong idea—
   Dante would know where to place him, spare
  ICE far down in hell
   but in this terza non-rhymed rima i will

  lock the Sheriff's non-remorseful soul in
@@@ signs & burning ampersands &&&&
  where it can circle
till he apologizes. Moves the men
   to Stockton or Nevada, profits will rise
      & as i told Alan

it's not that protests are useless, it's that
   some usefulness is too American.
  In tract homes nearby, black, brown & white
children lower their heads over games on screen.
  By the time this poem is printed the immigrants
have been moved

to what knows where & families
  don't know where they've gone. That's why we call
   some evil the non-soul. Centuries pass,
invasive but non-imperialist species are heaped
  in the field, useless magnetized
energy snags in the teeth of the daisies—

[interruption stichomythia]

—there's no such thing as political poetry

—*yes there certainly is*

—put it this way, there is no such thing as non-political poetry

—*yes there is, actually*

—what if the Sheriff sees that poem she just put in there

—*he is totally not going to see that poem*

Among Some Anapests
at Civic Center

The fascists have entered the town

       Sun like a late ripe peach

       City says no to masks

We go with the crows & the crowd
       A defensive line is made

The telomeres   all lined up

The state prepares the tear gas canisters
       (almost wrote teenage canisters)

The pronoun is wearing a mask
A defensive line is made

We go with G & H

Poets are often tired
We don't think the hitting will work
Grow calm   among the zeroes

Our house was a little too calm
       Our telomeres all lined up

Too old to jump over walls

A terrible beauty is dead
& the sun was tender upon us

We don't think the hitting will work
A defensive time is made

A poem is not a protest

Subject to history's impress

The telomeres all lined up
Subject to cosmic rays

Aw Aw awe awe crows say

The house was a little too calm
Was thinking of Nicolás Guillén
Was thinking of William Blake

Was thinking of very safe
Nice Germans in '38

We go with the crows & the crowd
Too old to jump over walls

A defensive line is made
        Subject to history's impress

We don't think the hitting will work

Changed utterly wrote Yeats

Sun like a late ripe peace

The State with tear gas thermoses
We follow the crows   *Awe Aw aw*

A defensive line is made
The house was a little too calm
A defensive line is made

We follow the crows & the qualm

repeat repeat repeat

Wiping Tear Gas Off Young People

They showed us the special area on the blanket off to the side where affected
people stumble & you take clean
cotton with the solution & wipe away from the eyes. A & i are wiping one
young man   & i'm thinking,
        he's just a kid. You wipe gently to the outside of the face. i can see really
there's no good way of doing it.

What is tear gas exactly? According to Wiki there is no significant difference in pain relief provided by
the different regimens. A study of 5 often-recommended treatments for skin pain Maalox, 2% lidocaine
with other things added, milk, water even some baby shampoo.
Avoid touching the affected area. Do not touch or wipe the eyes. The graphic of the molecule looks like a
dog with no front legs.

There's a tone i can't stand in political poetry; it's a mixture of drama & heroics.

It's impossible to escape having no clue.

The invisible is anarchic & meets cluelessly in small groups.

The protests are temporary but it's worse not to. To risk being outwardless——.
i worry about cops because they're young & one friend says, stop worrying about the cops.

Tear gas isn't gas, it is an aerosol version of bromoacetone or xylyl bromide.
A recovery of *vision* & the coordination of the eyes can be expected within 7 to 15 minutes.

If you're old you can almost fall running over barriers to escape the gas & when i get back to my car some-
one has scratched it. Bourgeois worry——scratched car. See, i'm getting into the tone now. It's the tone of
what a good person i am, the *i did all i could* tone.

Our poetry means nothing to the world. Yet millions need poetry, as Williams said.
Is poetry outside *the world* or is some definition of *world* wrong. Or not.
Is there a chance some of this will improve?

For AH & AT

Report on Another Encounter in Nature

After the EPA began to unravel, some students & i went out to read what used to be called nature poetry at a shopping center wearing Russian gas masks we had purchased on the internet. The students were brave. We were surrounded by grassy hills with so-called invasive species. There was a little buzzing from the edge of the universe. We felt everything intensely. Phrases sliced through the minutes then moved away through space.

At the Safeway a man came up to us—older white guy—& asked what we were doing there.

i said we were reading nature poetry outdoors because of what was happening to the EPA the EPA is being unravel & He said we would have to take our protest elsewhere. i said we were here as part of an ecology class. He said he owned the Safeway & we would have to leave. i looked at his Volvo, its gas tank full of screaming dead animals from the Cretaceous, a warm geologic period of "shallow inland seas," a phrase i've always found comforting.

We moved our reading a few yards away to some not-dirty western dirt full of not-yet extracted minerals & the secret water i pray to. Poets can bring odd thoughts outdoors. We moved to another town & read there. The rubber tubes of our masks looked like snouts of ancient anteaters dangling down over the pages or phones without being connected. At first it was hard to see the poems through the scratched eye goggles, & then we got the hang of it. We wondered how the gas masks had been used before this—just practice for war or what?—since they were sold on the web for $10 each.

What happened to our interlocutor? How will he live out his days, without poetry, with his features congested by fumes? If i knew his name, i could place it here in the poem instead of this text corrupter. ░░░░░░ Here is a little spell: *We will not meet him again on this earth. We will not meet him on the stairs of hell. We will not meet him in a place unseen. We will not meet him in a wishing well. There are books & beauty where we dwell. We will love each other in a dream.*

6 Views of Moss *Dendroalsia Abietinum*

(anadiplosis)

1//

Sky thickened windy probes near a zigzag tree. Tree
braying to push itself along. Along invisibilities
mosses curling appearances.   Appearances bringing
collapsed green, & the mosses   live among
acres of the self of earth, in a chain   of   thrilling glances as green
talks to the sky.

2//

ovate lanceolate

serate at the apex

cismontane

prorate abaxially

ovoid cylindric

tip long acuminate

3//

Nature is.   Is nature?   & you played with the
children among the mosses, their magic drawn
vertically from the book. As if in the drought,
a life   putting on
the third glove   of a blind harpist.

4//

In drought. Drought in. Nothing to be done. Is nothing? *Dentroalsia* curls
in matter & energy, energy & matter, in lignan, in the sloth. Bows in the

ssss the, the sloth, the true structure.   Drought rounds them. Is
there nothing you cannot do. Singing is common near curled mosses the
companions of trees. The singing is also material.

5//

By the body of the tree decoded, industrial. By the body of everything sacred. Moss bows
over the drying oak. The profit burns the body of the oak, $33,070,000 a year for M.
K.Wirth at Chevron, $23,500,000 for Darren Woods at Exxon, $20,691,139 for Joseph
Gorder at Valero burning the climate feet of the oak nearby.
i know this is polemical but there's not much time.

✳ ✳ ✳ ✳ ✳ ✳
✳ ✳ ✳ ✳ ✳ ✳
✳ ✳ ✳ ✳ ✳ ✳
✳ ✳ ✳ ✳ ✳ ✳
✳ ✳ ✳ ✳ ✳ ✳
✳ ✳ ✳ ✳ ✳ ✳

6//

Life & non-life end their attachments. Dynamic restraint among the beings.
            They could not stop or restrict the figurative.   Curls & pulls
& when you spoke to them after the first moisture the dead
ones could crouch & rise at the same time though mostly choose life—

[interruption stichomythia]

—*she just reread "season of mists & mellow fruitfulness" about 20 times*

—too tired to haul her old white ass to the climate strike

—*maybe just email the students thanks for organizing*

—maybe she should just start abiding

—*she's not the abiding type*

—moss on granite watching sea lions heading north

The American Burying Beetle

lives under only six states. With its faceted
black & orange head, it resembles those
outfits in the 1920s when the tombs
at Karnak were explored. The bug
belongs to the family Silphidae &
to the genus *Necrophorus*, & during
this awful year when humans are upset,
the American burying beetle goes on at
the brink of extinction costing the oil
& gas industry millions of dollars while it
carries the bodies of dead creatures
underground to lay its eggs
on the corpses, lurching &
arching its femurs & its tarsi
& its geometrical bright parts
to farm the rotting flesh for its
larvae to feast on, & when they
are ready, to fly off from. What
a wonder that so much exists
with no guile, that existence itself
has no rival & goes on as the thing
most steadily hoped for. When i feel
desperate about humans, i think of this
worker under the six states remaking the dead.

On the Molecules of Certain Ancestors

In mid-summer here   you can shake a plum tree & the fruit falls by
degrees.   My father couldn't   understand why
Californians   would leave   fruit on a tree.   On
evenings such   as these, when collectors of   fruit
might   be   listening & the unseen   is wide, i bring a
few plums   home from the tree   on the commons.

In the steamy Mississippi summer, picking   berries   on the family
        farm,   hogs nearby,   bristly wet snouts eating   dry   corn
accompanied by scrawny dogs, my brothers & I   walked   along in overalls
while our father   delivered speeches   about   family   & bloodlines.

The hemoglobin molecule   carries oxygen   from lungs to   the rest
of the body; the diagram looks like a bunch of plums   attached to the branch
        held up in summer,

hemoglobin pushing past   science, math, the poetry section   of the
        brain   & when i'm tired from a day, the bearable & the   unbear-
able,   ancestral molecules want to work harder,   four polypeptide chains,   the
two alpha   chains with
        their   concerns   & their   vapors,   their   orientation
        in   angular   minutes.

Those ancestors came mostly from Ireland, carrying hope, love, hate
        & work they   had been shown; intelligence & cunning made the
        whole tribe   energetic;

they farmed in the piney woods, the red clay soil with the   dense soft
        musty smell —;   it's not clear why poor whites   chose   such
        hard   resistant soil down there, why   they could
        take   land from people whose land it was; i'm not
        saying   anything new here; each family is different, but
        still.

The molecules of the blood work through explosions   & bells zinging around,
chains of history   fold to form   structures that
look like country roads   where nameless violence happens   &
on such roads,   in cones of the headlights,   bugs   hurry
only to   be smashed on windshields.

Recently i found a record showing a   great-great- grandfather signed up for the
Confederate army;   in fact he signed up twice.

One day recently i found a record that my great-great-grandfather enlisted
twice to fight for   the Confederacy.   Recently i
        found a record   in the family papers that one
        great-great-grandfather   signed up for the Confederacy &
        when his wound   healed he signed up again—
        i'm re-writing   that   but nothing

seems to change.   Dutiful man,   there   it is : : :
        the *history in*   *the context of his time* type thing,
        use the   strike-   through or   double strike-through
function,   ~~is there a way to~~   ~~get out of~~   ~~this.~~   Some
        readers   feel relief   it's not their
        ancestor.   Blood   moves the   system
between   useless   shame & useful fact,   hemoglobin
carrying   carbon & iron through   the body like   a peasant
cart of sticks & animals.

Poets want to look good in their poems. Some white readers in the group
rush in with reassurance, saying their ancestors were racist too. Let's look for "signs
of   progress":: "s" "i" "g" "n" "s"... Was thinking   about   Prospero
saying *This thing of darkness I acknowledge mine*   as *This thing of whiteness I
acknowledge mine* ; shouldn't rewrite   Shakespeare i know.

Certain practitioners of yoga can follow   a swallowed drop of water through
            their   bodies ;   i could not do that.   One of my older-
person   meds   needs you to   stand while the substance enters the
stomach,   after   which you can lie down.

The Mostly Everything That Everyone Is

My younger brother, a dutiful brave person, spends his work life studying the chestnut fungus *Cryphonectria parasitica* so American chestnut trees will not entirely vanish;

i'm especially glad for his work when i'm trying to get the skins off the brain-shaped nuts with their curly exteriors.

He was the cheerful child in the family, less seized than his siblings by the idea that to please our parents even somewhat we had to be almost or completely perfect at each task.

It seems his studied fungus makes cankers of two types: either they swell or sink. If sinking cankers, the wound kills the tree; it "knows" at its wound level what a life force is. Some genes that hurt the fungus help the tree. If the tree dies, the disease has become visible or it is visible because it dies.

Most of life's processes are repeatable—at first i wrote "all of life's" but that's so not true. Nerve-like structures fall from clouds only once. A shorter dawn sets in before the main dawn. Millions rise & go faithfully to work, taking their resolve, each person clears one throat, music is note by note,

my brother gets our elderly mother up, others in his family rise, he goes to his job free of self pity, the suppressed cheer of his childhood transferred

to his lab mates who monitor the tiny lives growing without human stress, hate, intention or cruelty but also without artful song so they dazzle no one.

My brother & i are as close as the skin on a chestnut is to the chestnut, as close as bark of the tree to its uses. When our mother was sad she shut herself in her room, & when she felt better she'd come out. You have to slough some things off, she'd say, loving us with decades of feral intensity.

He goes along, days pass through the mostly everything that everyone is, a sense of continuance is pulled from nothing, something produced when it can't stand being nothing, love in the experiments, numbers in the mystery, the healing of the wound, Psyche sorting seeds like minutes, a wound clinging to the tree, sometimes its fruit is food, sometimes the tree is nearly perfectly waiting

for BIH

1967

—the thought of electrons
giving off their light & their glory
  while every bit of otherness   is betrayed . . .

  i'm walking up Telegraph   during speeches for
Aretha Franklin & John ‖ McCain delivered
in eastern rooms where   ‖ caskets are displayed. . . .

  heading   to Amoeba ‖ for extra Aretha music,
    stopping to ask   ‖ the young man
               what is this & he says: it's a dispensary . . .

           & i say *oh for smoking pot,* — — & he says
not just for smoking, you can eat it, rub it on (big
pot smell puffing out, big contemptuous look from him

  & fortunately i do not start a sentence *in my generation*
      the wrinkles in my face
open their personal gates   to the lyrical

fog allowing color—).   ‖ Electrons pour into
     the brain till light ‖ brings minutes.
Someday there will be a happy medium (cliché

of a happy medium looking into a crystal ball—
antanaclasis—) Many shops are closing now.
  Is Amoeba Records doomed & if so, when?

Apple charges $9.95 for music you can't touch . . .
(Stop pausing, sunlight; there is nothing . . . . . .)
                    In 1967

Master Charge was on the rise . . . . . . 5.7 million "holders"
        then.   i was in high school. MZ
was born that year. Ché died in October, in Bolivia . . . . . .

The edges are sharp on violent   credit cards.
Older women are pretty   ‖ hard on ourselves— —
                (not that predictions matter but i never thought

i'd be 67). You're not going to be able to save everything.
        There is pink sunlight with   electrons falling
                during the minutes.   ‖ We   knew

little but couldn't imagine   ‖ killing children for
the revolution not even rich children . . . . . .
So many shops are out of business now—

A first draft of the poem flew past as i felt
   a western draft—the word *draft* meant   state
terror in 1967 . . .   The day   ‖ i started this,

a draft came through my wrinkles . . . Students weren't
watching McCain's or Aretha's funerals . . . . . . Still. Getting
        through the day matters.   The young pushed along

down Telegraph with   ‖ electrons streaming through
                inverted parabolas of their headsets   bypassing
their souls   into consciousness . . . . . . They don't seem to

mind   or feel the rage   ‖ about the bloated fees to Apple.
So much of this kind of thing.   7.3 % people of color
were without jobs,   3.4 %   of whites without jobs in 1967.

Slick apartments go up in Berkeley while electrons
fall apart   without commitment to those heavy hadrons—
‖ One must have a mind of mycorrhizal netting to regard

the chthonic lining   of carbon life
        under the avenue   & to behold the universe
as a skein of feeling dots   where the energy is pure

& whispers to the dead . . . . Full of shame
    i held the LP with RESPECT by the edges
& played it w/ my friends. Can you even imagine

no internet??   Respect us, internet —*homoioteleuton* =
off rhyme) When she sang R-E-S-P-E-C-T even the boys
‖ felt it. Creatures & colors dash past the closed shops,

our students   dash along,   their grandparents
‖ from Philippines, from China, from Oakland, from Guam,
they brush past.   There were 2,975 corporate

mergers (an increase of 578 from 1966 . . . .)
‖ These wrinkles on my skin are feared by America
  ~ ~ ~ shall i cut my face behind? Do i dare to be a peach?

    Electrons speak in negatives
at the southern   Sather gate.   The pot shop
‖ bodyguard showed no respect for an older woman. . . . . .

Our innocent secrets were commodified,
      pot was 10 dollars for a big fat sack—
we called it   *A LID OF DOPE*   in 1967—

MLK said the U.S. was the greatest purveyor of violence
in the world.   During the funerals doves & crows
   call   in slightly golden teardrop squeezed amounts

(Don't slide back—guard the partitions)   Ho Chi Minh's
trail would not be known. The human   ‖ hope is to be known.
   Everybody is wanting to   ‖ be respected

& not to look back with oblivious eyes.   ‖ To R-E-S-P-E-C-T
over & over & hope for understanding . . . Pampers
were introduced & began to fill   ‖ the land. Poisons

built up but so did delicious kissing.   The Vatican took back
the thing of no meat on Fridays   help for the meat industry?
Bodies opened for us truly. . . . . .   ‖ TL defiantly & with

      fond smoke on her hands
passed banned books under the desk. *Ulysses.* Miniskirts with
pantyhose so you could sit with your

legs open (Minutes, thank you
   for those) Humans were not stable then. Never had been.
      When Ho Chi Minh asked that the bombing be halted

      not only did they not stop, the U.S. opened bases
in Thailand to be closer for access . . . . . .
      Plagued by the sense of inadequacy & dread, we

desired to make history; love was less common then, so we lay
in the grass while the bombing continued. Sometimes
   did.   Read a little modernism.   In 1967

art saved us, then as now. As now dread is followed
by humility after you give a poetry reading ("as now. As now"
is *anadiplosis*, which sounds   ‖ like a James Joyce character.)

Wore gossamer   & paste   ‖ plus circles of actual daisies.
We desired to make history. Love was less common
before that   so we made it up.

                                    ‖ Some white men got beaten
for one inch of extra hair but black men had always been beaten.
Bombing continued.   ‖ Sometimes did. Some

babbled in   English class   ‖ on LSD, some
died before adulthood.   ‖ Adulthood before died . . . . .
Mining tar sands had begun in Canada. Canada was where

peace boys ran to. More anadiplosis. (Some repetitions
    free you if you can stop them in time.)
 . . . . . . McCain was bombing for freedom then

captured.   i threw no rocks till 1969.
    First televised bombing, the path winds
through the jungle, path with bombs fully falling

on the villagers, what did he think about while being
tortured for 5 years . . . ,,, electrons in his brain
flowing toward   the Mekong . . . . . . Students barely

    hear about the bombing of brown people now
        or the double O of oil & opium
plus famine plus profit. .   In 1967's

version of R-E-S-P-E-C-T the *sock it to me sock it to me*
was an expression we didn't understand.
     Some songs get you through the day & that

was one. Aretha traded irony for power. . . . . . Irony is
  a defense for the sensitive unless it's overdone like Walter
Benjamin says about surrealism   & then later

the whole capitalist horror came down to: you can sit
on your ass if you're middle class & feel helpless . . . . . .
    In Europe students felt   ‖ helpless & rose up.

  White kids were   ‖ clueless about whiteness.
Rubbed butter on the skin to make it tan. Lead
  in the paint, lead in the water . . . . . . De-halved ourselves

& joined the crowd. Poetry was ‖ secret dope. Boys were
    an anarchist   ‖ then a pacifist then most of
  a communist. Girls needed heroes of course & we tried

     to fix   our looks but never   pretty enough
then got undressed in the desert without body shame while
a rabbit chewed delicate   ‖ grasses. The CIA

gathered 300,000 names . . . TL passed *Ulysses* under
the desk. Arrests. We had many minds with one soul; it
held everything. Berries, herbs, homemade pies, ok call me

Arwen. The U.S. said Viet Cong will be chased into Cambodia
& they were. They were chased. You were organizing,
    i would have   loved you then.   In 1967

Dow Chemical the napalm
the toxins the Roundup dumped in Nimrodel . . . . . .
That year a door was cut in my face. One of my wrinkles is

named capitalism, one is named Barry Goldwater &
all of them are named   *don't complain, just work more.*
    i never forgave McCain not even seeing his head

swollen with cancer surgeries because each time he made one
of his smug speeches i thought of the people he killed,
    he lay in Hanoi Hilton for five years tortured

but celebrated for "not giving in to Communists" & when
        they released him   he started asking
the Pentagon for   thirty more years of bombing till he died.

On the day called today when i started this poem in 2018
    i saw her picture, in the Times: red high heels,
ankles crossed in her casket, ‖ the gleam entering

wood & satin. Minutes pass ‖ through us one at a time,
music passes,   turning   ‖ dysfunctional families
into miracles,   history ‖ suffers, mothers suffer,

    Hegel says dialectical but there are
more than two. What percent of our 525,600 minutes
this year will immediately turn into history?

What percent will become radiant twice fallen infinity?
As i walked up   Telegraph before the first
    draft of this   i saw ‖ a house fly sitting on a piece

of pizza trash rubbing all of its elbows during Aretha's
service,   ‖ which i watched on my phone.
It is not safe to look at your phone   while walking.

OK change the tone, tired brenda, & give the readers hope.
Humans have radiant intelligence, they have a chance,
    Say: No one is like you.

    Say: We need others badly.
    Say: The alleged left has no heroes now,
            that's why our heroes are electrons &

leap, they leap   in their light & glory.
    Am trying to imagine useless revolt.
Am trying to trade resentment for energy & love,

we get older, it gets wiser,   you & i drive
        from the west with curry leftovers in paper bags.
                My tercets have fallen apart, Dante;

little takes little takes little takes on history. *What shall we
        do now* young friends ask & i say care . . . . . .
as the earth will return to electrons from whence it came.

The small rails ‖ s in this poem seem to be space & time
        when minutes seem to line up but then don't.
        We wrote in our diaries & kept

            excellent records, backward
            forward history & beside,   R-E-S-P-E-C-T—
        Aretha was teaching people how to spell—

III. There Are Many Women to Cherish

. . . women who have gone ahead, **Lorine Niedecker,
Barbara Guest, Audre Lorde, Theresa Hak Kyung Cha,
Ana Cristina Cesar,** & **C.D. Wright** among them

. . . women who work at their art, **Ashwini Bhat,
Nancy Bratt, Frances Lerner** among them

. . . women who work with others, **Sahai Burrowes,
Margaret Handley, Kristin Hass, Louisa Michaels** among them

Winter Daybreak Stanzas
for Our Daughters

The gibbous moon sits swollen among
the god amounts, passing an elsewhere
    of those who know our daughters.
Experience & peril are both experimental,
        from the root *per*, to risk.
    i call on figures whose atoms
        might protect us while deer feed
on ferns with elderly brown spores.

    Our daughters were born when our
lives were in chaos. After that,
        we were able to love. Now
they live past our reach but
    we're sleepless when they have trouble.
They spend days sorting toxic minutes
    from calmer layers, & their honesty
        is rare in the working world.

    One doe scratches an itch on
her back, jaw moving counterclockwise,
    her smart nose reaching far into
the dawn. Her fawn spots merged
    with sunlight long ago & will
circle the tree forever. The perceiving
        mind is restless but can surround
the infinite stress of human love.

for HA & MN

59

The Closing of a Midtown Bookstore

Even in the twentieth century   sometimes a peaceful glory

i worked for a decade in a bookshop first as a married woman then as a mother

Dust settled on the words   in mid-city near a curly gate

Light held matter there & they spoke to each other free of gravity

When customers came through   the books leaned

They shared their shining skins some days

i brought my baby to work some days
Some days she was sick & slept under the counter   She was a friendly baby & barely cried

When she was older she played till my workday was done

Sea of faces is a cliché but our customers were celestial & ordinary
Some were unstable
Spirits of dead & living writers held us close

Literature & the rest of thought lived in the shop secretly
As the great caves   go undetected for centuries   subject to *drip drip*

& when explorers find them
Light lies down in one direction toward the entrance   waiting to be described

i spent most paychecks on toys & on objects to quiet parts of my mind . . .

i bought some books i knew i would not read

Customers came in leisure or trouble   & when the lean years came
how did the shop manage   Dust & tiny flies with serrated wings died there . . .

Through what desired codes is knowledge made

Now the shop will not reopen & some night force comes soaring
& whispering over the body of my first love paper

& of my second love   paper   & of the mute love paper

for CC & KM

A Pattern of Minutes During Illness

Our friend was struggling with her
cancer while her calm met extremes
in the brain below the follicles
of hair setting in, or into
the arms of others, while her
body that had often been joyful
rejected the celebrated chemicals;—; she didn't
glamorize a so-called acceptance process but

kept moving through the rounded minutes
of her days as bees in
her yard of double-faced roses sped
into a wheel of notches at
the center of time, or into
time at the center of each
rose. It wasn't that our friend
had grown wiser, she just didn't

choose despair;; & sometimes she had
better days or skipped whole segments
in ways we couldn't understand as
if she worked on an abstract
pattern for her friends. No individual
piece made sense but there were
arrangements to be made among humans
& she was committed to making them.

for NS

For Our Students Reading the Odyssey

A little hope existed   in the fate shapes

Then you remembered   how alike you were to earth

Mercury minutes   not stolen from time

Each phrase gleaming   with a color of the senses

But history hovered   while the leader spoke landishly

But a goddess had bathed you

But the sailor had fallen   from the house

& when barley had been offered   for the dead

& when the invisible   had been eaten by the visible

Much was offered   sticky sugars from the pines

The so-called lower elements   still had eyes
& spoke to you   or could have

The Working Sister of the Muses

The muses were distracted so they called their sister in
She flew from the east to the west to the middle
Someone had told her to bring the arrows
Someone had told her to bring libations & bolts of lightning & the charts
She arrived with good cheer & wore her hair long then
She brought a sketch of the weather & the wild hearts
Thus she worked for decades among star-gazers & word makers in a town
with green summers & a smooth black angel
She lived among those transfixed by sorrow & desire
She never told them art is the same as not art because it is not
She never told them not to write the wildest thing in the dark
She never gave the sleepers any reason not to sleep
She never told the silver children not to play
She knew whom to phone from the maze when the word makers made
trouble & when the lilies were held high

In summer the underworld pushed up seeds & her tall lover grew them as food

In autumn the pages swelled & shelves were built & word makers failed & some jokes did too

In winter the hero's epic shield was displayed & it told all stories except hers
She could see her face in the shield though she tried to have no face

In spring she rose early to walk when each leaf caught the sun

She celebrated prizes & mourned the deaths after their songs had gone
She did not cast down the lightning

She did not stamp the sad harrowing ledgers
She loved the abstract ones the happy ones the ragged & the drunk
She told them it was their energy & their dream energy went on .
She was the rosy-fingered sister working for the dawn

For CB

Lines for the
19th Amendment Centennial

1

The century speeds along
Sound & dust & color & light

Clouds speed over ballgames & wars
Nerves hanging off them   Women watch

early election results   Stressed-out women
in hats & choirs   Women sitting under

suburban stars   Women with husbands
or wives   Housed or unhoused women

with herbs or guns   Women with
friends & cats   who are always tired

New medium or old   to the world order
Who pull their masks tightly after the fires

2

Over 52,000,000 minutes. . . . . .since the 19th
Amendment,,,,,, Over 26,000,000 women voted
after that ;;;;;; mostly only white women because
of the poll tax. . . Now let's just think about that . . .

There are 53 minutes in a micro-century:::
We place extra dots as eyes for extra vision: : :
There are two periods in the 19th Amendment
i place them here . . for women

who want to be women or don't
We were dodging the little zeroes between mystery
& meaning.,. history & hope   We were walking or
driving i was flying left till my left wing broke

3

Some women vote with armed guards   Some
have their forearms stamped   The branches

of the oak are breaking off   The particle
spirits are being used up   There are two

men in *amendment* There is *gerry* in *gerrymander*
There are eyeless vans from Amazon outside

like hearses bearing the corpse of profit
Some women do not like to vote   They think

the revolution will come faster   The land
is blighted Muriel   Is weather better if you

order online   Is earth's orbit polyethylene
i thought of not voting but there isn't time

4

The great dead teach the living not to hate or
to try to love imperfectly   At what point

did voting really begin   Wyoming (oddly)
was the first state   Some practiced law

but couldn't vote   Seneca Falls 1848
Lucy Stone abolitionist could not vote

Impossible to reconcile   what you want
with what you are . . . . . . i'm voting extra

with my shoe   Applying text corrupter
here for how long justice takes

We leafleted in 1968   Come out of your
house & stand now   You count too

5

The right of citizens to vote,,,"'" shall not (she'll not)
be denied   or abridged /// ;;; ;;;

(i'm adding 46 marks of punctuation for 46
years until the 1966 Voting Rights Act)

by the U******nited States or by any State
. . . . . . >>>>>> & the names will survive

Frances Ellen Watkins Harper,,,,,, Hallie
Quinn Brown .   . Mary Church Terrell

& Congress shall not remove cage kill & undo
citizens because of age ability gender race

etc. Some vote despite perfectionism
Messy marks   in tiny tiny hollow squares

6

i voted first in 1972   tear gas   My Lai   Weather
Underground   mostly voted against things then

Agent Orange   the draft   had gone
to the trailer park with leaflets   We were new to

the Pill   nice sex or terrible   with skinny stoned boys
Smog in LA   We stayed in the dorm   burning incense

Can't remember who i voted for   ankles showing
under the curtain   Metal bar on top

like you were taking a shower   Mostly always voted
Just had the habit   Once wrote in my friend's name

The land is blighted Adrienne   Absentee ballot
i tear the numbered stub then i mail it in

7

My seatmate on the plane   speaks first
older woman   taking care of herself   dental

assistant from Virginia   i suspect she voted for T
Friendly over-60s whiteness is our commons

Our legs stick to fake leather   flying over some
cleaned up rivers   still adding carbon to the air

Her $12 cheese plate dwindles   We talk   We both
love our jobs   She puts small instruments in patients'

mouths   i use small instruments with patience
She's going to Las Vegas to play black jack   Laughs

Our story sails along   inside oblivion
Our electrons   speed inside oblivion

8

The yellow minutes of our coasts
The saturation of our voices

Centuries of women sick on a ship
Decades of women sick at the office

Women in tents in a marketplace
where the orange canary sings beside

the masterpiece they made   At times i hear
the queen of ants   At times i feel the great

dead choose for us to keep unreasonable
joy   & revolution in the craft we made

We fed refusal to the storm   to live
in the dream   in revolt   in realism

for our granddaughters
for Adrienne Rich
for JB, AH, ER, JR

[interruption stichomythia]

—this seems to be another one of her unruly projects

—*she writes poems not projects*

—seems like people always ask what's your next project

—*she writes poems*

—project is a perfectly good word

—*she's talking to William Blake right now so please shut up*

In Some Senses of the Word

The spirits stand round
in their bristly ovals. They don't
really know what to do. A bobcat
hunts on the oblong
hill, its tan hunger ruffling
the saturn grasses. A day
brings velvet fog to the warm
ground. The wren with the *n*
at the edge of its nest
makes all sounds eat
from earth while lost things turn
& circulate. Stuck

in your golden thought, dreaming
of apocalypse or blood, you call
to the dead, not sure now.
You call to the body, much closer than
a place. Your brain makes a chant:

At the edge of the wood
it will know where to turn
At the egde *of the world*
they might know we're to turn
At the edge of the word
we may know here to turn

for coven51 & CAC

Taking the Sunflower to the Mountains

i held our sunflower up as we drove
past fields of former sunflowers,
            past Margaret's house & rows
                of dead dry stalks   quite prone
like summer's pale accomplishments.
    It had had a good life in the yard
& would scatter   lavish seeds
beneath the smoke from western fires.
            Our flower looked out from the Prius
            while i whispered in its ear:
                Where my sunflower wishes to go
                    (from Blake)
                & *You were never no locomotive*
                    (from Ginsberg)
o o o o o o

        . .

        .   . Our sunflower looked off-key,
        .   .   it had a broken stem & wouldn't
make it to the mountains whole.

``````  But it had captured oxygen in its beaks
            & would stretchhhh
    its golden aura
            to the ground.  It's necessary to travel
            between realisms.
M & i had discussed how women & plants might do
the work. The flower kept watch on its
last day, guarding every opening & door.

**For MR**
``````

After the Fires,,, In the Mountains,,,

The spirit seedlings do their yellow best.
   The sister seedlings move to the cold ground;
they join the feral mother
dressed in ash.   They join the feral
brother dressed in ask ;;;
......///° · ·.

There came a time attached
to the cold ground. Golden-crowned.
Some agencies moved humans to new
metal boxes. Flies on
   corpses of the question marks.
      Fucking stupid leaders—excuse me,
stupid fucking leaders—said profit hotel
attack mode. Earth said,
the large gods are lucky
   not to exist. Unimaginable
     conflict as families apply for
       little scraps of state money.

At solstice, without despair,
when nights are long, we study
the classics that halt in the middle
of action. Humans loved life very much,
it was never just us vs. the sun king
or single minutes vs. all of eternity.

after SEM

S / kin

of old woman walking   from a lake   shaking   after swimming

with *if & is*

      venules in   her seven-layered   s kin   stratum cells

her

                    stratum corneum   *stratum lucidum*

stacked up layers

stratum granulosum Lamellar   walking from   a lake at risk

purple platelets   body's

      mini-cities of troy   trees of consciousness   bent from chill

lake less clear than

a Wednesday ago   water warmer   than decades before

post-cancer site

somewhat

        s kin of a white woman   dripping with cold   medul-

la cortex   sheaths   hairs bent   bulblike   past eternal present

human s kin   miracle   to be known   lake less clear
          than decades ago   oil glands   hair roots   plunged
granular   cells of keratin
dropped as she swam   2 million-year-old   lake unplanned
doing eternity or never
     on its own   nearby towns   subcutaneous   motor oil urban run-
off   still swimmable water
                 warmer than planned   wider than Tuesday   older than
joy   older white s kin
so oddly set   water   seems invincible   lake   much warmer by
one degree   a woman swam
     her s kin loves science   stratum spinosum   s   kin has wild nerves
came cancer   decades   don't know when
stratum basale   algae growth   in the lake   lost thin s kin
melanocytes   her pigment   history's advantage   dermis   Merkel
disks   Meissner's corpuscles   recollection when   touched by

bandaids borrowed makeup   radiant sex   said to her lover's   sweet

pressure   *mm nice*

lake   absorbs scaly   salmon   brought in   a decade ago

tiny shrimp

species   further declined   EPA spent 47 million

some s ((kin sloughed off

inclined blood   chagrined   upside down   tubes of   collagen

corporations sell

embarrassment   old s kin   different surfaces   aren't embar-

rassment

lake with more

future   since 2010

blood vessels   5 yards of them   4 yards of nerves 650 sweat glands

curled   cobra tubes

at work   her nervousness   god forgot   to turn the science off   sweat

sheaths   hair follicles

skinny tulip bulbs   under surface   1,500   sense receptors   secret pathways

with   yet yet   yet yet yet   thinking of

              1oo oil glands   nerves   touching air   after swim-

ming   good it   feels something   a word is   the s kin of experience

spinous cells   sweat glands

hypodermis   good type of fat   papillary   capillary   Ruffini's endings

all that

              walking from the lake   goose-bumps   real goose nearby   s kin

rises   near friends

      no longer rises for   the national anthem   rises   for love rises

with

                  picnic   with moonrise toward   the rest of

them

for SO & GS

History of Punctuation on the Face

We love punctuation we love it on our
Faces between our eyes the commas
On pages Slashes & virgules by the noses
The deeper ones called smile lines
The history of punctuation on our faces
The not smooth now colonized landforms
Try ageless skin revolution dot com
An internet pop-up says between news
Botox could fix your punctuation
& we don't want service worker bacteria
Injected in our skin some of our sisters
Said naming wrinkles after the drier years

The history of punctuation in the west
Men were reading silently Women didn't
Read of course They were accompanied   • • ••
By the lyre & strings Construction
Workers do not whistle anymore
Because of punctuation on my faces
When i think of the invention of signs   . . . .
When we think interpunct the small plump
Dot made reading easier We welcome
Extra punctuation over time Women   ,,,,,,,,,
Sat up high in the arena No signs
For when the gladiators killed
& on the wrinkled earth the animal   ~~~~~~~...

                                                        ~~~~~~~...

The interpunct kept pace & thus the scribes
Began their sense of inner pacing
At what level did experience begin
Thus began the sense of inner facing At
What degree do Botox creatures stretch   ^^^^]]\\\~~
Marks designed to make reading easier
Weakness happens when the muscles   ]]]]]]]]~~~
Fall They invented the diple & the period   ,",,,",",,
At the Grand Canyon we saw wrinkles
Up & down from the Precambrian
What's so bad about granite wrinkles
What's so bad about punctuated women

The parenthesis was added later
Grief Botox may cause side effects
We won't accept a corporate account
Of our skin We do accept the long Pre-   ^^^^]]\\\
Cambrian The feldspar in the west
The punctuation in the texts Monks   ///////\\\\\\
Placed marks in surviving manuscripts
Mostly not coming from the author   ~~~~~~~~
Aurelius noted he had inserted marks   ))(()) (())
Others appear in the 4th century
Not hopeless only adding pauses
Metamorphic commas on the faces   ,,,,,,, ,,,,,,,

Marks had been inserted to show forces
The diple with one dot of traces   > >. > >. > >.\
The asterisk appeared medievally   ;;;;;;;;;
The *punctus exclamativus* & by then

Human surprise had been invented
Experience on our faces & once when   ((((((~~~~~)))))
We were hiking down into the Precambrian
Granitic structures Huge Vishnu Complex   }}}})))
We had extra experience A reader suddenly
Allowed to put the marks in The printer
Made the right to put emotions in   ]]]]]]]~~~
When he left her punctuation deepened

Only some languages develop commas
Some faces Some agreements have &   [[[]]&/// <.>
Time makes other lines within the sense
Of sense He started leaving her when
She grew Precambrian around the eyes
He was very going to leave her then he did   \\\   //
Another started naming wrinkles after times
She named them Valley of the M Heart-
Break Budget Protest App When you see
An older woman on the street a reading   ///////\\\\\\
Of her beauty starts No stretching skin
Smile lines built like the Precambrian

She began to think of reading on her face
Read wrinkles like experimental poetry   `~`~~``~``~
Lines backed up from the Precambrian
Wrinkled earth over a billion years
His new wife had no lines at all
No timing had developed on the skin   ————///\\~~~~
Isadore promoted silent reading
They're kind of beautiful if you don't
Allow a corporation on your skin   (((((0)))))

Song of the ridiculous Well you really   ]]]]]]]]~~~
Had a good run of it with all that
Happened to your skin & women
Looked down to the ground we love   ~~~~~~~~
                                                          ‹‹‹‹‹‹‹‹

Older ground becomes so rich & rare
After Botox she couldn't whistle well
Zoroaster granite's igneous intrusions
The corporation needs our shameful self   ((……..,,,
In her divorce the wrinkles deepened   (((((/////
Individual wrinkles named for lovers
Young & older writing adding time   ??}}}\||/
To it the commas of pure pleasure
After great pain the Precambrian
Some sense in the experiment grew
The pattern of pure pleasure grew
The measure of text is not pre-death

They call it facework now an understretch   `````,,,,,,,,,
Of tiny creatures in the skin The western
Lovely friend afraid of smiling now
Did Sappho know about the interpunct
My wrinkles are beside the earthly years   (((((/////
Traces in surviving manuscripts where
Monks inserted one of the centuries
The actress had a good run of it he wrote
They called her wrinkles tiny flaws
Emerging tiny flaws above the sweat
Glands & the sensory receptors In our
Grand Canyon the comma is the door

What is your favorite form of punctuation?
My favorite form is the almost pause
To have some extra time around the dream
Not dream of youth (Poor Botox creatures
Chained into our friend) O semicolon
Why hatred of old women not of earth?
Why no hatred of old canyons Why no hatred
Of the Valley Why hatred of the women
Doing nails & women eating, teaching
Nursing babies walking talking bent
Like commas Why do the aging women
Apologize until they barely even talk ? Asked

The semicolon & it said don't be ashamed
Of your skin i asked comma it said
Don't be ashamed of your eyes i asked
The virgule the parenthesis the dash
The tilde the umlaut the macron They
Said don't be ashamed shame shame
i asked the ellipsis & the period
The exclamation & the question mark
To read the human woman's face &
The signs said take your time The pauses
Bent & heard, as did the quartzes &
Cracked feldspar faces of the canyons

There are the marks & runnels &
Rivulets, scratches & of exiles
Skin, sex, age, capacities. Oh quartz,
Ah granite, basalt, lava, faces
Stay with you. They remember

You. They made signs with laughter.
Old women we remembered you.
Remembered the wrinkles under
Cities. The faces ours, full of pain
. . . dots & lines, & whines;;; faces
loved in suffering & gladness over
all the earth—!!??~~''//. .;;,,]]{{

[collage essay]

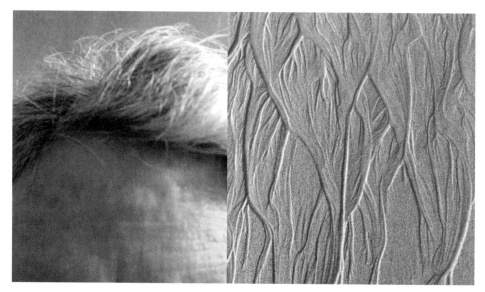

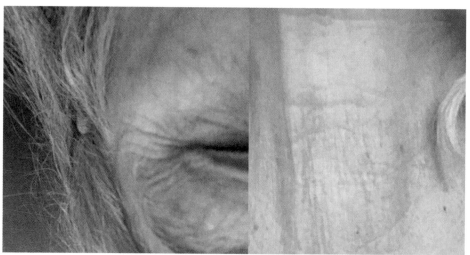

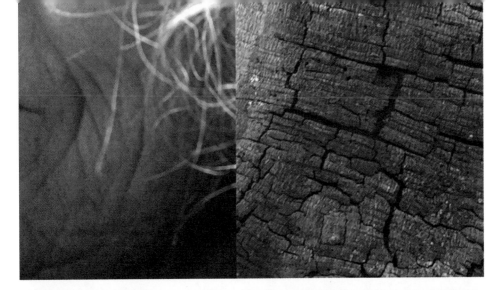

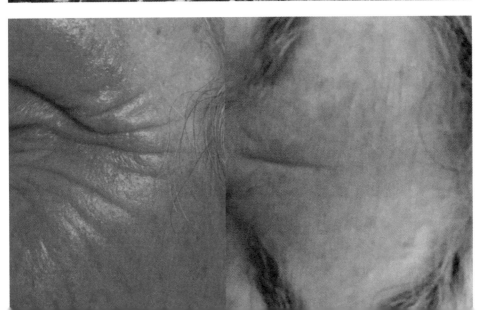

89

IV. For Writers Who Are Having Trouble

(12 poems & 3 interruptions)

All I can suggest you already know: start something else
& what you need should come back to you.
   Charles Altieri (from correspondence)

... For a minute say every letter of every word
but slowly.
   Fred Moten, *The Little Edges*

... walking along a cliff's edge & a peek over reveals my self
falling back up ... Patience promotes a calmness with the waiting.
   Joshua Zelesnick (from correspondence)

A Feeling Right Before the Feeling

At sunrise the deer eat
pieces of the quiet, they eat spaces
between the quiet
   & the sounds—;
     & the numbers on the calendar
lie flat in their boxes,
   they leak through tiny holes
      in the minutes,
      evenly so, so evenly,
an active sense, before
   the sense was made . . .

There, now, opposite to set down,
      the agreed-upon, the shape
     of the obvious
   drawn by an earlier
    enchantment before the new
       anxiety set in:
   the workers are safe;
  the terror stilled for an hour;
a lover's outline, dreamed or imagined,
   before you read the one-page book
  again, what was that book,
it had no copyright—

& what was before?
   a life, the dazzler, the dark,
    the singing dust, it turned

when you turned, it orpheus-knew
what you forgot when you took the bowl
of burning time across the room—
& if the previous is closer
to you now, should you
look, doesn't matter if you do,
you carry the some of it
with it, out into it—

for LG

On Days When We Both Travel

Everything is so stressful. Was it
always like this? Air full of
        bitter flecks from the fires; friends
in despair over violence & money;
for many, a feeling of being
        unhinged, or if not unhinged, one
screw taken out of the door.
        You got up & left before
dawn, taking your frayed black bag;
        i left soon after that, afraid,
going the opposite way. Daily this
  curtain between death & life then

K's baby is born just north
  of here. Now the 4-part call
  of the crow snags gravity from
stars that crashed millions of years
back~~ the 4 floats in
        my blood like a broken chair
in a flood. On the plane
        i read the work of friends
on earth: abstract, intimate, grounded or
rough, difficult, delved, simple or winged,
  sometimes poetry can't do enough or
sometimes poetry can do enough—

                                                        for KP

[interruption stichomythia]

—what about meaning

—*meaning is the third half*

—someone asked if her book is negative or positive

—*she should refuse to answer*

—she already answered

—*what did she say*

Concerning the Meaning
Molecule in Poetry

Long ago a man told me, If you write poetry
        keep your subjects small;

i was a tiny skinny girl at that point . . .

Much later, i heard a meaning molecule
in the call of a dove pretending to be an owl in the pine,

a song-speck circling in a thought throughout all time
        (like the man said, *extremely* small)

traveling from before literature
through the blue centuries until quite recently

when a radiant instance of the unknown

    paused our bafflement but kept
that little meaning absolutely elusive, & erotic . . .

for AC & NS

The Child, Finishing
Fourth Grade Online,

when his mother asked,

"how was that?"

said,   "odd."

The Scattering of the Lyric *I*

—when the lyric *I* is   falling apart,

                                                              (i

      the muse arrives at the end not   the start,   (i i i i

when the lyric i has fallen apart;

                                                                 (i

where will it end   when it stops its route,

                                                            (i

    the half-self, the quarter, dermal
cells of the root

    an orchid putting one foot   (i
               on the pot,,,

    a dot   on its skull,
what becomes of you,   when the water drop

falls down & not up,   silence   (i i i i
      exile, & cunning,   periderm,

      cork,,   (i ii iii

, , , , ,
             the tail   (i
     of a lizard   put back
in the sun,

    hiding in shadow,   venetian assassin,   (ii i
                                                (i i ii

whose muse is absence,
    whose dream is a weapon—

The Photograph of the Black Hole

in the *New York Times* looks so much like a writer's doubt when the writing
falls into an unread zone, an active nothing where nothing breaks up then falls

into many more minutes than that, a never-having-been both dense & scattered
that rests near the always in the great dark.

You write in a calm room under a curved light where oblivion finds a home.
Someone has suggested you meditate.

The doubt also looks like a tunnel where a late train arrives & a worker
loads a package addressed to a third person living nowhere.

Of course you're tired. Your art is burning inside you & your art doesn't burn
for committees or for decorated disks, it is a ceaseless moving energy.

What on earth were you thinking. Of course you can't let go.
Of course you have to go on writing even to barely exist.

for DM

Her Map Might Change Its Arrows

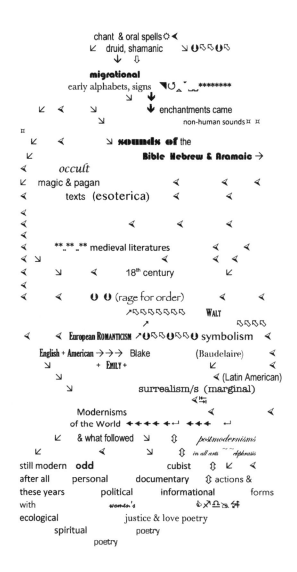

chant & oral spells ✿ ◄
  ↙   druid, shamanic   ↘ ᘝᘖᘝᘖ
       ↓   ⇩

migrational
early alphabets, signs   ◥ᘔ‸˜‿ *********
          ↘   ↓ enchantments came
↙ ◄   ↘   non-human sounds ¤   ¤
    ↘
¤
↙   ◄   ↘ **sounds of** the
↙
         Bible Hebrew & Aramaic →
◄   *occult*
↙   magic & pagan   ◄   ◄   ◄
◄   texts (esoterica)   ◄   ◄
◄
◄   ◄   ◄   ◄
◄
◄   **·**·**·** medieval literatures   ◄   ◄
◄ ↘   ◄   ◄ ↘
◄   ↘   ◄   18th century   ↙
◄
◄   ◄   ᘔ ᘔ (rage for order)   ◄   ◄
        ↗ᘖᘖᘖᘖᘖ   Wᴀʟᴛ
        ↗   ᘖᘖᘖ
◄   ◄ European Rᴏᴍᴀɴᴛɪᴄɪsᴍ ↗ᘔᘖᘖᘔᘖᘖᘔ symbolism   ◄
English + American → → →   Blake   (Baudelaire)   ◄
    ↘   + Eᴍɪʟʏ +   ◄
     ↘   ◄ (Latin American)
      ↘   surrealism/s (marginal)
                     ◄↤↴
    Modernisms   ◄
of the World ◄ ◄ ◄ ◄ ↵   ◄ ◄ ◄   ↵
↙   & what followed   ↘   ↕   *postmodernisms*
↙   ◄   ↘   ↕   *in all arts* ~ *ekphrasis*
still modern **odd**   cubist   ↕ ↙ ◄
after all   personal   documentary   ↕ actions &
these years   political   informational   forms
with   *women's*   ᘖ↗ᘔᘖᙢ
ecological   justice & love poetry
    spiritual   poetry
       poetry

[interruption stichomythia]

—why did she put that nutty page in there

—*someone asked her if she has a 'lineage'*

—she'll drive off the normal reader if she does stuff like that

—*there is no normal reader*

—she's always driving off the normal reader

—*send it to eternity magazine*

Dear emerging, pre-emerging & post-emerging poets,

Lisa has asked me to write you a note in case you are feeling discouraged about some public aspects of your poetry. It's hard not to be discouraged when there is so much ignorance helplessly displayed toward our art. It is not surprising that you feel overly sensitive when poetry —or your poetry—is ignored. Books of poetry are left off "best-of" lists; they are rarely reviewed in major venues & when they are mentioned, it might be only for some perceived aspect of marketable content. Try to get past this. You are bringing your rare imagination & your love of language to the culture that needs those things. Poetry is not a "specialized field." It has universal & eternal value. It is something most people start writing when they are children. It is what humans read to each other at weddings & funerals. It takes us into vast spiritual adventures. It enacts original dreams. You do not need to dumb down your art or ignore a century of modernist practice to please what is sometimes called a larger audience. It is not a poet's job to simplify the mystery of existence or its lexicon. Is the life of the soul ever easy? When you feel downcast, keep in mind those who have encouraged you along the way & write for them; imagine a stranger who may be reading one of your poems in secret someday. Try not to think about people who are writing facile things on the internet. Remember the radical ancestor poets who have gone before, especially those who received less acknowledgment than they should have, those whose genius was insufficiently recognized. Their poetry provides excellent company, as does the work of great living poets who offer inspiration & consolation. Read across aesthetic lines & identity groups, assembling a varied canon. When you feel paralyzed by the pointlessness of temporary fashion, or when dull or predictable work is lauded, try new things that will surprise you as you work for the joy of the process, remembering that all a writer needs are four true readers & one of them can be a tree. Never look at your phone when walking downstairs. Do not destroy your body by self-medicating under poetic stress. Just write new poems & read them to your community. Keep the ego in balance because the ego project is doomed to fail. If you don't receive the rewards you deserve from "the outside world"—and you very likely will not—try to celebrate the good work of others; hold love in your heart; work for justice for humans & non-humans & keep writing. love, Brenda

For One Who Paused Her Writing

(did a spell with 24 y's):

Took the *y* in *they*

                Took the *y* in *you*

  with particle spirits   being used up

Oak tree blew lightly   leftly   loudly

    Ancestry   of moth mystery under sky

       cloud clotty   hours yet away

Varied *y's* gathered   for a day
      Till nothing betrayed her

   Not ardency   unyellow yet

No one   messing up *y y y*

   No one telling her to stop

For MW

To the Poets of Myanmar

(epanalepsis)

1.

Sun not yet here is the sun. Nothing to do with because. The scattering
of the spirit, lime green hills. Women among the jeweled threads.
Margins now at the margins.   Inanimate not seen of itself.
Torn daylight's features, near a staff.   Palms, casuarinas,
      whispering pines.   Teak & cuff of the colonel.   You'll be understood
in a different way.   Sun not the sun is the sun.

2.

Spirit scatters
against the white building's spirit.   Prophetic spores,
      unmeasured hyphae. But the hour is coming . . . but the hour is not yet come . . .
& just then   +++++++++++   & the moon not rising till noon,
& the rice fields still being seen.   Signing the document
      the same as not signing the document, in spirit.

3.

Our enemy lies even in our dreams of our enemy.

Your enemies lie even in their dreams of their enemies.

Their enemies lie even in your dreams. We need

to forgive the enemy. . . . & we saw this thought was not of them,

our enemy who never thought of us,   though

we thought of them every single day, our enemy.

4.

Shadows under 6-fold Buddha rays 8 hairs of the Buddha
The rare red panda falling 2 months or more
* * * * * * * * * * *
* * * * * * * * * * *
Numbers falling in & out of the election   Crows falling
on a lump of coal   Rare red panda falling 2 months or more
* * * * * * * * * * *
* * * * * * * * * * *
& the shadows hiding one darkness from another rare red
panda in the shadow in the brain of the poet   of shadows
* * * * * * * * * * *
* * * * * * * * * * *

5.

Impermanence & suffering.   Floating lamps, boat
        on the river, spirulina out to sea. Mold colony spores find themselves
in pigmentation of exile, in the grain, free dream of the child

holding the grain bouquet, spores of the mold on the grain,
in the poet's brown room of the prison, their
journey will cover your music the impermanence.

6.

Sun hope sends its antic breath around
to the back of the page. As wands of mosquitoes love
each other
poets think of each other.
Shadow says to the poet, Tend to the night my friend my own.
Tend to the night gently my own, under the moon another sun.

for "The Poets of No Name"

::[an artist's sound, between the Farallones]::

—then the universe
dropped down,
coughed a world,, trussed

a deeper dark
single
caudex of sound,
a wonderment,,;

      the invisible
    is active today—; cleaves
     to the skin,   twins

thy tired shadow
  to hear

        begin, begin, (being
        with the *g* moved in (

then sea birds
  could swing through
every irrelevance, inexhaustible

numbers,   a typical radiance

for MS & EK

[interruption stichomythia]

—what are we

—*some sort of granular spirit concept*

—speak for yourself

—*i can't, i'm a we*

—we can do whatever we want

—*no we can't, we're the spares*

Winter Song for One Who Suffers

The stars stand up
behind the day. A known dove balances
on its claw
at the window. A cosmic incident
of darkness has begun

        &a mild excess of beauty
      will be offered to the dead,
      which they will eat. On a hill

the wise man serves the people,
your thought splits
in half when he speaks of the old
revolts, the return
of apocalypse, motive & advancement.

      A soul can crouch
       a long time while the heart
        expands to reach its edges.
What is missing past the glitter
of the harvest?
             Friend, you chose
to live. How? You did. So many
choices, not just two, encrypted
behind the mystery of the sun,

then the hurt was set aside,
  indeterminate chaos
called in by love.

V. The Sickness & the World Soul

24 poems

This bare and simple infinity, or the absolute notion, may be called the ultimate nature of life, the soul of the world, the universal life-blood, which courses everywhere, and whose flow is neither disturbed nor checked by any obstructing distinction, but is itself every distinction that arises, as well as that into which all distinctions are dissolved . . .

Georg Hegel, *The Phenomenology of Spirit* (*The Phenomenology of Mind*)

Write the thing which thou has seen
Revelation 1:19

. . . the mysticism of descent . . .
Fr. Vincent Pizzuto

. . . between now and the apocalypse . . .
Chris Nealon

:::[a ragged white moth passes by]:::

         —had no first line & the epic
was museless except for one elderly moth
         flying through as the spirit of history.

The sickness was also flying though it was not alive.

When would they meet?   & when
we thought of the world soul, how should distances apply?

Past papered windows of locked up cafés, the quartz in the desert
         & the fabled silicon mind meld, past the uninsured . . .

Mosses on buildings looked like themselves,
         crowded but separate, social cell walls & stems—
each with a certain commitment to survive . . .

i, a poet on the island of a thought, with love nearby
lit a candle throughout spring. On & on
the little beasts visited. No
666 for them. The rat & bacteria & the sparrow's gold corona.

The ragged white moth of history flew over landfills &
         the anti-sorrow of the flat few,

2 wings, 6 legs or 4 wings, depending, flew with the *m* of our minds
         or the missing ones, its faraway moth-babies in the drawers
         quietly eating the sweaters of our mothers,

& the jeweled threads of the protein wove the sickness
    looking like life or death, though truly it was neither

& parallel to that, in the green springing hills the grace-footed
dark-haired spirit of the will-not-end—

3/18/20   214,010
4/15/20   2,054,218

after DJR

[at a hospital: in the east]

protein;

integer;

    a without-
resting-place sequence of
   memory's smallest unit
picks the lock in its luck: (which?),

a stopless future grabs the list: the *wasn't*
        next to *the might be*
& the ragged   world soul
goes about its business:

      crisis of history,,

        throng of forgiveness—

3-19-20	244,517
4-16-20	2,116,698

[little breath circles   all across town]

i thought i saw a man bent over   but it was a road sign;
    i thought i heard *deploying data management systems*
    but it was just sounds in the mind—;

        Dr. L woke early   breathed & put on
      a blue sheath; Dr. M woke on   earth, logged in, & counted
a fringed flight of numbers. Some woke old & alone & when

    they died they were ours. Unprecedented was our word.

C closed the shop & the books read to each other, as we have written,
    the data driven . . . ,

    the yellow dress left at the laundry
recalled its one body
& the single lemon on a branch hung like   a Wednesday.   Radiance,
    what is your intention. We lit a single   candle, not twelve;
        & the world soul floated over
the bored children with their handhelds & the adults with their own
    beasts & their own apocalypse
      while the sickness passed by
    going the other way in a yearning chorus of fragments.

    Intention, what is your intention.

    Wasn't there meaning
among the jeweled threads?   A ~ C ~ G ~ T

(you can buy the RNA sequencing kit online for 4,000 U.S. dollars)—

we could hear the great dead with fires far off,
we could hear the ones we love, the singing flame—

| 3-20-20 | 258,003 |
| 4-29-20 | 3,127,519 |

for LH & MH

[: : : at equinox, same 12 squares, window : : :]

short logics:
      what was hoped for?
—sun & mist!   Down garden   stairs

      where immensity
is low, crenulate (to send an anxious
      thought, to workers, masked)

   if radiance persists: say yes . . . Then a crow

      crossed through the death breath siren's path,

  over mosses a color from a book sent by
a friend: & you think *celandine* back to her,

      (a green from which
   amethyst could be launched . . .)

3/21/20   305,202
5/1/20   3,271,961

for KK

[stayed busy inside   moments of not]

       —stayed busy inside   the moments of not touching,
(irregular chirping   in the rosebush: a tiny broken
coffee maker, maybe a towhee)—. Planes sat idle
     (please, let's stop calling them birds) . . . rat, owl, fox, newt,
        raccoon, squirrel, bee, finch, skunk, flea;
            each family had its own beast,
blue skies returned to Los Angeles,
water recovered, the moon forevered. Roses stared in at us
as if yearning,   belief is not irrelevant to this.
Silence of the violence, what we were made of,
        weeks into it, changed little,   though
       more people were cleaning their own houses.

There's still time for the moth of history to fly
through snow-stars falling
from events we remember clearly
standing under the magic & tragic blooming of proximate trees
in our centuries Beijing Berkeley Berlin
the apex of blossoms
& the ache of our love beneath them inside each silence
the being of numbers
breathing with us until we nearly could not bear the immensity
but we had to
inside longer numbers right
to the edge of their suffering

3-23-20   379,236
5-6-20   3,835, 831

:::[the invisible is full for you]:::

Days are calm,   for some,   fox
        in its closeness   X's the ground,   dawn's

        hushed forms,—rat, deer   launch a few vowels;

a spare soul   sent out   early to be with them:

in the tale, the seventh seal is broken: silence follows;
        many stopped breathing—last week

        past comprehension . . .   creation writes in us
       to be life,   snatched from the hand;

the invisible is full for you,
past lowest   mosses;

hyaline   sky,   wise science,   the love   fear

        passed through   full for you now . . .

3-24-20   407,485
5-8-20   3,941,371

122

[in the split gardens   irrational hope]

i saw the clouds go by in used lab coats.
i heard the neighbor looking for her cat.
    The hour is come, the prophet wrote
the squirrel has no apocalypse, & shakes
  a gravid branch—
consciousness in high places . . .

quietly we walk quietly
   past closed storefronts,   buckets out front,
     roses outpace the thrips: no average realism . . .

             Oh sleeper stay with me, for
               i have buried my alphabet
             in a garden of zeroes—

They ask us to make videos to comfort people
(hands of the dying on the glass)
so i prop my phone up on a basket & record a poem
for elders & inmates—
       to what end, a voice asks, the "system"
     is sick, whatever the system is,
then the voice between mystery & meaning
uncancels the journey,

    inexhaustible light
has entered us, sufferer, right out
   to the sea of gray stars—

3-25-20   438,749
5-15-20   4,444,670

[poem on a birthday::: in shelter]

(shared

birthday: plump squirrel in the yard
              scolding the finches)

—so creation   retrieves being,,
how?/(as):

     ♪   lipid-covered   protein—; ;

breathed,   you felt
a soul pass by,

                              ♪
     ♪   a thread   commandeered
                 to exist

          encountered nothing   (destroyed that)
       encountered never   (destroyed that)

     3/27/20   509,164
     5/18/20   4,822,430

                                                      For LEL

[trance poem   with the gray stone]

We traveled between   dimensions in spring

mild weather   medium depression

white tents at the hospital   propped up on stakes
a few   desultory carts outside   like Europe

number is all   wrote Baudelaire

was holding   a spry gray stone   given to me by A

could hear   the crow the fertile eye of the rat

i said to my companion   There

a prank of orange poppies   fluttering on the hill
apex of the white moth   over a landfill

4 animals of the apocalypse   but calmer

number is in the individual wrote Baudelaire

vessels in the road   wrote 6 plastic

felt some souls pass by   those i had known
some yet to be known   Here they said

bees had been coming back
violence had not returned in full force

breath of life inside our spirit

& fog passed by   byssoid   wooly
each breath   a soul we loved   like women's art

a soul   a fluttering between worlds

[depending on what you mean by that]

3-29-20   634,813
7-2-20   10,716,063

for CDW & FL

[asyndeton of adenine cytosine guanine uracil]

in warm pools　　4 threads　then more

a billion　　years　breath　moss

fern　　lamina　　lizard　dolphin

parrot beak　　intention　love　poem

feeling　　latent　　music　thought

spear　work　law war　bread from

wheat　time　towns　the scroll

the week　robes from linen　books　screens the

death-crown　the un-always　the always

death passes by　deer　jay　short candle

brought in　jazz　　Stéphane Grappelli

flame flickers　　pillow falls to the floor

4-4-20　　1,197,775

7-22-20　　14,982,567

:::[when spring dusk   fills the garden]:::

& bees visit   the stamped flower

apiphily
the moth   falls back over

an incurved serrate   oblong
    toothing petal,   toward

denticulate   invader berry's leaf,
a second thickening;,

yes,   & no
    death crown

    found this
body yet,   referendum
on existence:

time, born
from itself,   then it knew

    how deeply you loved

how the universe met its proof—

24 moving
spine bones—

anchored   dusk swallowed
the why not . . . the hollow
holds   the body,
borrows effort
    calm takes place   but how

4-11-20   1,762,943
7-24-20   15,526,057

after George Oppen

:::[lines on Easter   during the sickness]:::

—it was so

quiet in our hearts,
many molecules barely   coping now

(trying not to put the life force   far from contact,
& my white health
at what cost?   Whose hands set

bags on the porch. . . .)

The dear priest   does communion on Zoom

(in this church   he can talk about
his husband)
sets   a thin plate
over the wine,   not serving it—

4-13-20   1,929,485
7-25-20   15,949, 267

[for the workers   suddenly less employed]

carousel man who helped boy off the zebra
nail salon woman who chose lavender
N tried to get an icon blouse to fit
bookstore worker
other bookstore worker
scraper of ponds
baker of seedful curled pastry
dream worker
brogue-talking fixer of heels
quiet man who played with tigers
maker of fantasy tubes
music-maker counter of frets
pilot dealt two bad hands
dirt worker propping up heads of poppies
volunteer too tired to be praised
meat packer listening to Joan Jett
teacher watching old brothers online
mother saying stop imitating me please online
caretaker of shallow stories online
placer of the seven flames
philosopher who loved freedom
library cleaner with spray bottle
bike repairman reading instructions
seer of air through the spokes

4-18-20   2,292,303
7-28-20   16,495,309

::[untitled]::

i asked unknown dark energy   that pulls
     the furry light   between stars   back to
the start of time   if everyone
has to meet again

killers   who enter houses   without knocking

     does the sky have to forgive cars

do monarchs forgive the spray

should day forgive another day

4-20-20   2,414,370
7-29-20   16,760,915

:::[to the voice of the age]:::

They gave up their fear of sincerity

They gave up   their decorated nights

Evening birdsong had folded into chalk

Evening shadows grew less white

We'd been faithful mostly
to our own special tribe

      Couldn't keep the burned forests alive

Of the beasts of the apocalypse   one was light green

It was a dream   We didn't choose that

We chose the rat   the cat   the fox   the past

& when we sang to ourselves   the song went

      What is the voice of the age my friends
What is the age of the voice
     Adenine Cytosine Guanine Uracil
The voice of the age   is a fragment

O sea of glass   Cart of straws   O air

        round as the love of moths

      Hard to forgive certain centuries my friends

The age of the voice is the choices
The voice of the page is the voices

O love song   in an old blue cart

Wheel of ciphers   wheel of eyes
Wheel of beauty   code & blues
The voice of the age is the voices

4-22-20   2,590,125
7-31-20   17,321,394

for GGOB

::[in a place   with no light]::

In the sea   some creatures   only eat / eat only

        when sediment falls down

On soil   angiotensin enzymes   change to
running   the sickness   has no legs

When you write there's a storm in each sign

Eyes   near each candle
Size in each light

All this life   there you are
trapped in yourself
surely you can
forgive a few more people

4-25-20   2,822,003
8-2-20   18,003,985

[_____]

5-26-20	5,512,055
8-2-20	18,013,985

:::[smooth black stone   has seen everything]:::

Taaa taaa of helicopters   during the protest

Did the century wake us   or was it something rare

Please stop calling window breaking violence

Cop's tibia   fibula femur = violence

No ventilator   for the inmate   = violence

                Four pillars of apocalypse
          Holding up the loneliness   this

Gray loneliness   at the heart of awe

Flowering of flames   during the curfew

Parallel light in the skull

Away it goes   saved it goes

The well-being of a few irrelevant as Pluto

It's hopeful to see crowds in the streets

Come demon flames   chthonic sisters

Rise from what we   have not learned

Racist centuries swept into oblivion

When will people start forgetting

   On the desk a rock from the railroad
   into Auschwitz

It is shaped like a human ankle

i recall my normally calm friend

Sobbing there near   *ARBEIT MACHT FREI*

Stones & art stand by

Powerless to stop all this suffering

6-2-20	6,288,167
8- 7-20	19,111,123

for JH

[chiasmus with all the other animals]

Curled thrush song staggering   over moral tally

Number is all   wrote Baudelaire

     Fox kits hunting   solitary voles

So many beings here without despair

From a box of words   called a room
We heard   a protest among the distances

The pall   caul   crawl   through summer

Struggling bees   not yet out of work

Cities were running out of sidewalks
       where men could sleep

     Human life   on the high fade

    Didn't see plovers   but saw yellow tape

Didn't see whales chasing   dots of krill
   Some might make it north
    Captain Ahab   chasing minnows now

Compared to what
is this our earthly fear

Roadside mosses   seasonally moist rocks

Unfailing dirt   arriving from a star

Straight from   its lifelike origins dear

Love   keep love   at the crossroads
Of doing nothing   & nothing doing

Before the ignorant machine opens
Briefly & always   to another life

6-3-20   6,479, 562
8-3-20   18, 283,575

:::[the voice of the age   chorus]:::

The voice of the age is
the silence   The age of the voice
is the ragman   The choice of the age
is the violence   The voice of the age is a fragment

!!!!   !!!!   !!!!
!!!!   !!!!
!!!!   !!!!   !!!!
!!!!   !!!!

Stars rose from the edge of the world
            i heard the great dead say
you can write anyway you want
     it's all relevant

6-5-20   6,658,334
8-10-20   19,876,301

for TEM

[pinched   nerve   in my white arm]

—& the nuthatch   opens its   micro-meadow
of *rsk- risk rskrsk -*   near the neighbors wall— hyphens of not
letting absence   get in its   way;;   twin fog   draws over

the mostly-bolted lettuce garden   its imperial chalk;

the several-months-long-now pinched

nerve reaches down my white
left arm
& out the hand into what feels like a bowl of asterisks . . . fireworks &
a few explosions across town, protests,   helicopters join the firing of
of the synapses; the feel of minor
chrysanthemums of
numbness travel to the table where an article called "What
Ordinary Citizens Can Do"   lies flat—

      Across the water, , , a night nurse trying
          to catch a bus that's not running,   pulls up
her stocking while holding   her phone with a picture of her
grandson holding his mother's phone, playing police games;

       it's early summer,   nearly solstice;
    each half song in late wide light is true;
   600 million alveoli in the human body . . .

my friend D said pain is a portal . . . Jarrell said it is pain.
Another voice said   can't you love some
part of this world purely   not just in
                    preparation for the abyss?

6-20-20   8,804,972
8-10-20   19,876,302

for DH

[the hive interrogates   the helpless hum]

dawn force, then

some numerals:::,

                        you saw   near here
a wasp hive   in a tree,,,   a mummy head
            12 brown holes with   legs dangling from
its paper

world, like
the light of the mind hidden, as it often is,
like a wide unseen,   pushing
past the ego . . . What was the humming

hive thinking?
                Your friend was trying to stay sober
going to meetings online—   she said,

            there *is* an "it is" that isn't lonely. The wasp hive
            swung like a lantern of
            here you are. If
            Hildegaard saw the thousand eyes in the tent
surely you can know another person.

6-21-20   8,954,471 cases

for MS

::[the fourth part of a triptych]::

—of the pollen.... unaccountable

gold entering tufts of bronzed *when*,

the unconsoled / consoling mosses—

(but you had your childhood!)   upper margins of it
    „ „ the little beasts,„, crouching   [secret rat]

with the you still missing—(o –o-o   o) of owl – 2

now!   [how did you   come to poetry

maybe you   can't recall?] scattered

the proud   of the (with the)—no, not
being   ill! rumored & convolute

like mosses in filtered light „, „„ & now,

messenger thread   grasses, comose stems

near a city hospital, in white tents —for them

garden of: flutter   to breathe in?

o   knowing nothing else?

of asking,, sediment   in pines city cones
no seven seals   of apocalypse   to break

    under the fur of stars

unboundedness (o past sickness—!)

forgives debt, [the garden told itself,   recall
rumors   of goodness]

of a great strange life past sorrow

[untitled tableau]

The soul sits beside its box of oranges.

The century goes along,   the tyranny,
the dazzle,   the executions of butterflies—

life molecules make memory-shapes,
adorned   broken or blunted . . .

the replica of the virus
looks like a Christmas ornament from Walmart.

Some days   you could barely read.
Some days you wrote from your strangeness.
        Some days, you imitated those who imitate you . . .

A pressure   mounts through chaos.
The protein   takes down human systems &

you are somehow supposed to make art
of dreams or childhood,
of history's injustice or love   so here you are
in a room by yourself

& they've left you   with a spoon & a pencil:

        Just try to eat with this pencil, they said.
        Now try to write   with the spoon.

But the breath between
numbers will never run out,

& you know that you know that you know
so there's that

& the minutes pass,   each odder than the next (or, if

not odder, at least   passing   & the next—)

6-26-20   9,628,658

VI. In a Few Minutes Before Later

12 poems for **Robert Hass**
including a half alphabet of endangered words

1. Be ready to evacuate. Take only a single vehicle to help reduce traffic jams. 2. Make sure that you have at least 3/4 full tank of fuel. 3. Park your vehicle: (a) In a driveway facing the street, not in a garage. If you have a driveway gate, leave it open or (b) on the street in the direction of departure. 4. Keep vehicle keys in your pocket. 5. Keep plenty of drinking water in your vehicle. 6. Load time-sensitive medications into the vehicle. Unopened insulin can be stored at room temperature for up to 28 days. 7. Keep an emergency kit & first aid kit in your vehicle. 8. Pre-load your vehicle with Go-Bags, keepsake items & small toys for your children. 9. Plan to evacuate before a mandatory order is issued especially if you need more time. 10. Help & pick up neighbors who need assistance evacuating.

> **For more information on wildfire preparedness, visit:**
> **www.ci.richmond.ca.us/3627/Wildfire-Information**

Time is short.   Time is short.
   Michael Sell (from correspondence)

There's light on the spectrum we can't see.
   Ira Flatow, Science Friday

Escape & Energy

The hills are burning;   they have burned & will burn.

Sheets of lightning over introduced grasses
       whose arc is low,   trees leap
              across highways . . . ,

young men tending the flames all night,

lightning totally unprepared to come back strikes
       the long awns
     of non-native grasses,

fire in service of pure light, not consciousness.

i'm an older white woman who hates to sleep;;

      my bad eyes see things
that aren't there—at least
on this side—

             when the third eye
        is active, as now, an energy

leaks between worlds;

it's then i feel helped.   It's then we are helped.

i pack the car while   fire workers try to decide
which among them,   whose worlds to save.

It's the end of empire.   i wish it were the end of empire.

My love is a good sleeper;
        his mind rests in its great gifts,
               & we will hold hands at dawn—

The ground of being is changed

What gives calm joy?
a presence beyond
    peril, bringing
        the don't choose to
boundary layers pulled back:

   ,,, ,,,

      mosses crouch
    in their assembly,
unmourning the morning;;
a robin's
 arrows spin over them
from the mouth of time;:

in a few minutes
before later
  at the ground of being
breaching nothing
    where methane's
      wheel can't reach:
  love's neighbor,
fond knowledge, no
stranger, not mourning

    earth's life,
life's earth, love's life
stronger than danger—

Escape & Logic

i hear tonight the great horned owl,
    4 gray notes
superior to beauty.

Come to the window, i say;
                      (my love can't hear & i can't see;
we trade senses throughout the day)

Last night 12,000 lightning bolts upon the earth—
(*upon*= such a stiff word . . .
      where did we put our glasses?—*upon* the dresser) . . .

packing the car, folding color while workers start what's called
"back fires"   for culms
    of late grasses   where the ordinary is swollen, breathing

ash,   the neurotransmitters making a pact
with the logic world   allowing
entities ,,,,   allowing fury   at the end of towns,

      racist profits of extraction,
        Blake's angels   moored   in their fury,

  cultures in migration, unredeemed upon the earth . . .
Here in the garage
  smoke specks   for company,   packing *items* . . .

some pines   save seeds   now burning to grow,, ;
there comes to mind   June Carter's "Ring of Fire"
& her sister's cool rendition.   Chrome aperture of ash, ::

garage spider:::   Did i help my love at all? i worry
i did not.   Thousands
   of days he helped me.   Loading

 family papers, a doll the screws fell out of, my
mother's   extreme red high heels   from 1968,
the brain snags in the settler cells, acetylcholine, glutamate,

   pumping between minutes. My love sleeps in
his nature   through phone alerts.
   Mostly we have not failed each other. . . . . .

foxtail grasses burning,
 the bossy squirrel sleeps nearby, in nests of justice
& spirit threads,   to put its slumber in.

We learned names of western grasses \ \ \ \ \ \
   that burn now, *non-native*
fescue & brome, *Avena,*   we took a class,

  kindly but sanctimonious white people in gray clothing
stooping with hand-lenses   over   species
brought by colonizing soldiers centuries back, grasses

speeding   to their doom,   young firefighters
& entities—   (Is a group of angels
always called   a host? Never a *flock*?

„, cherubim, seraphim, orphani . . .).   Among   angelic
    hosts   Rilke cried,   sending his daughter
away;   some poets

       take solitude too far . . . Western angels
drop their wings like termites in the heat;
  some   are pushed like coins in a vending machine,

      organic angels   aren't sprayed. . . .
we're helpless   with wind picking up, our own
  collective   to the edge.

There is indeed a mystical consciousness
where we will meet
but how we arrive   we have no pilot for.

Loading pounds of paper in the hybrid—
  a poem is also a hybrid, \ \ \

mind & miracle, wrote D.   Intensity gathers.

When the young ask: what was the most difficult
thing for you as a writer:

the most difficult thing is to love. Actually, the most
        difficult thing is to feel loved—

Punctuation at the end of time

You will love each other
till the end of time   (totally
a cliché but)... seems
like time might have more
than one end: : knoblike
structures on butterfly feelers,
(butterflies have them,
moths don't...
Rhopalocera, clubbed horn, sort of
micro-clocks telling monarchs
when to migrate & so on, twin
apostrophes like "   or ',

one on the distal side toward eternity,
one toward human life);; sometimes
the end of time is in the middle

as Lyn's essay against
closure indicates. Also noted is how
finality in some poems is scattered
to make nano-seconds as when
light strikes one of two nothings on
biramous branches of the righteous oak....
if you loved a person well
it lasted   till the end of time,,
after which, it continued—

Escape & Song

The owl calls all night. Its
       puffy wings turn outward   where leaves turn
          outward too. *Extrorse. Eccentric.* Axis off-

          center as in most poetry. Q: Which angel
raised his flaming sword? A: Uriel. We give the world
our descant songs . . . June Carter gave "Ring of Fire,"

    to Anita to record   ,,, Johnny made it a hit . . .
Rilke didn't live long enough to
      stay inside the spell of someone else. When my

love asked me to climb the parapet of doubt & jump
i nearly missed . . . nearly failed a great chance,
     fell several times within,   *who if I cried out*

in northern flame,   spirits fly backward
     through the damaged eye,

over the ashes of California,,,, over common waxberry.

common snowberry to rescue seeds consumed by
fire, *Synphoricarpos albus*.   Song produced by
  a tiny wren with endless woven songs . . . when

we make love, it teeters in high *C*, double *M*,
we've been so scolded over—!
		red alerts in the phone, pack the car,

		fire takes the land back,
		we don't own it,
tomorrow is not another fucking day,

mountain lions come down often now,
—not exactly climate migrants. In fields,

		prickly gourds getting by on their own moisture.
A small percent fits in the hybrid.   Family albums
			with crinkly cellophane sheets

mended with scotch tape.
   Thousand of letters with gone thoughts—so many
		humans living in what used to be called

		comfort zones
		  beside species left to mourn,	unhelped by
trends: what shall we do, the young ask . . .

	videos of cars flying just in front of the flames—
   What are the angelic orders, Rilke.
Cherubims calling us are actually hawks.   In Exodus

   the angel appears, the burning bush & so forth;;
our epic love has flaws,
				the fear of not-love

overcome   by the made love—
i hope he forgives me some of my bullshit
& our ashes hold hands in the dust,

that our ashes might mingle in the dust . . .

In the garage, an orb weaver spider

lines its web with trash & shines like galaxies.

Love & Myth

Many love poems are yearning.
Some are funny like beards on trees.
Your time on earth is brief, so speak
       your love without delay.
  In some the names are changed. Through
time   your angel passes by, & dust fills up
    the back of your eye,,,
you pray to a god of nothingness
to release you from the contract. Maybe
  rethink that. You were sustained
by color, your love was not the longing type
not fluted shame, not post anything.

    Some could love through change,   they
breathed the evil
    down. Oblivious
      love might be renounced . . . *Get it right,*
          Get it right, sang the vowels
          & live with your love in time,
            & thus they lived among
          breathtaking forces,,
        near the righteous oak,
       dispersal & contour, near
      the prickly skin of the gourd—

The Themes in American Literature

The great theme of American literature is

1.   the search for home
2.   the search for love
3.   the search
4.   great themes are not American

When the woman smells smoke she packs her college notes
in the trunk

Packs the children's art
funny ceramics with superannuated glazes
Packs the fossil collection from 60 million BCE
Broken camera someone   threw at her in DC

Packs   quilts made of overalls in 1923
Centuries of women of all
            skin tones sewing & praying   under their breath

                    the breath for women is low
(& when you fold up the frayed thing
made by a woman's hands
        please don't ask Did your mother work?)

Some families don't save much

The woman packs her letters from the Age of Paper

Maybe she met her love in a book someone gave her
She met him between the lines of a letter   He lived
nearby & came to drop a package for her then husband

stood in the kitchen handsome & kind
stood in the kitchen   now filled with floating ash
seemed to listen with his whole mind

Did she hold her baby then   A story began to form
There's always a crisis
Great love starts in a crisis   density
of ash settling in the air in the folds of things & wings outside

        The wasp gall turns
        on its side in the night   abandons
larvae movement   replaced by escape through punctuation

Marks like the shell of the gall in a field at the end of time
● ● ○ ◉

She packs the letters they sent
He was in charge of summer
He was kind to her child

If there are specks of other people's houses in your mouths
If you were the settler or the victim of profit
Now ashes of houses where some were loved & lived their lives

Their lives are in the oxygen of many people now

Each time they pack   an epic is remade

No no no no no more empires please
No more stepping over prone bodies when wearing genteel yoga pants please
No more fracking in the Pacific please
No more climate idiocies

There will again be great cities where dirt sits down outside
            50 million years of it
There will again be syllables to mingle with the plants & float
            to their demise

To angels who won't return in the same way but
            in an ashen voice of crystal time we say
before our kind shall disappear & your kind & their kind

& thus was the seventh seal broken & someone was making
                        a meatless dinner
& thus the lovers lived in ordinary glory/danger/glory/danger

air from the owl's wings falling over them

Those who had loved before them & would love again
        & the glabrous leaves made traces

By day the orange glow from the ring of fire blocked the sun
        let it be said
            their bodies kept the chaos out

            The alto moon of the smoke alarm
        glowed above their bed

while earth survived its humans   through the tear/tear
in the back of each eye
sensation rushed with all its needed color

& dawn pleaded for a boat not made from threatened trees
        not wine dark
not tragic & never distinct from literature

During an enchantment in the life

Do you love a living person
        absolutely? Tell them now.
In a half-unwieldy life you made, under
the hyaline sky, while the dead
  drank from zigzag pools nearby,
if they saved you in your wild incapacities,

  in timing of the world's harm
in a little pettiness in your own heart while others took
  your madrigals in shreds to a tribunal,
        when others said you should feel grateful
  to be minimally adequate for the world's
triple exposure or some tired committee . . .

  The ones who love us, how do they
break through our defenses?
  We're tired today. Come back later.
Their baffled voices melting our wax walls
with a candle, the ones who understand
what being is—the glowing, the broken,

the wheels, the brave ones—
  they have their courage,
you have yours,,,,;
      when you meet the one you love,
it is so rare. When you meet
the one who loves you, it is extremely rare.

Escape & Speculation

Sometimes decades go by in my poems. Maybe the next book will be
about centuries.
Little lights come on in the great heat. The colors gather strength.
In the epics there are catalogues.   Pack the eraser made
        of rubber from Burma,

pack the first ex-wife's
        holiday cards, pack a baby's torn shoes, stones from Berlin,
boxes of drafts that housed irrelevant suffering

(Is suffering ever irrelevant?)

Pack the paper snowflake made by a child. Which child's
snowflake goes in which box . . .

Each angel rushes in differently. Some sprint.
i call to the twelve dark fields.
        Sometimes it is an owl or a spider. The doomed world
is redeemed through fire
but not through burning plastic. Is the doomed world redeemed through fire?

Amorites, Perizzites (a rural people), Hittites, climate migrations
from greed & ignorance, we hold
    our humanity with the dry stalk, i talk to the spider who has golden stripes,
who is not dangerous,
        Araneidae Araneidae

angels crouch in the back of the eye passing unannounced
through modalities,

pack the second ex-wife's assemblage of pictures—

where is that weird green saturn cup she gave him? Let's carry it to exile.

We'll write the book of great cities, we will write Nineveh syllables,
Ninevah, bombed with U.S. tax dollars—

pack the hearing aid batteries.   The small ones cry out & are sent on.

Let us in   *Let us in*   say the hierarchies, the seraphim,
the cherubim, the bees, the aphids, other winged contributors,

       thrones & principalities, 6-winged flies,
    take a left turn
    at the hills where noons are married, over the murmuring

      gold of California,
you are ash, you are ash, the chrome notes
    of acetylcholine dance over the cleared space,

    over purred anonymities—

the trees align through smoke & believe themselves,
involute song: *the taste of love is sweet*, sang the Carter sisters
    & we fell into the ring of fire.

Our storage shed has orange doors.
Were we enchanted by the wrong things? Not really, no.

When we cried out the angels were already
    speaking in specks   to every living thing,

                    as M has said "the flecks
chipped off the soul by the voice of my enemies—"
& what if the ash spoke to us.
& what if the healing was not what we expected
& what if we save as much as we can in the columns
& the small ones cry out & are sent on . . .

i'm not going to say where we'll meet. It's a secret.
Let's meet under the owl.

This love stripped my doubt away.   If i die first,

if he calls out, if the children
          call   i'll be hitting my slippers
like tulip petals against the wall of heaven,,,

(remember i've told you heaven is lateral
                so keep
the windows closed because of the ash—)

Doubt & Love

       The owl calls all night.
Poetry is another example. Were you
               disappointed? No one
   tried to fool you. Did you write one line
somebody cherished? It wasn't
between love or work (that was a guy thing).
You make art through the exceptions.

The destroying wind starts up, the new purifier
      H recommended traps particles so you can breathe.
A prophet has prepared the double share, some stuff
        can be saved, surely matter
    matters & it does, they do. Each night brings fear,

     communities pick through rubble,
in the lost world: no
justice for human systems as we wear the robe
     of sparks & contracts for the species
          are called in,,. . of course we could
be doing more. Daylight summons one
    striped finch, new
minutes from the vault. We lived
    intensely & intensely joined. Had you
     lived otherwise you would have missed
       the great thing, more perhaps. Your fate
      would have written something else—

Escape & Exeunt

The lights come on in the great heat.

Where shall we take our stuff?

The storage unit down by the water has doors like metal fire & chunky keys we can't lose track of.

Others arrived with large carts they couldn't steer.

Where are you from we'd ask in the elevator.

The planets gather in alignment over the houses & the people gather strength.
Boxes loaded in our cars again then taken out

when fire again does not come for us.

The rat & the squirrel crouch at dawn & late finches come with dull
         fiery heads from the lenticels.

We called to the 12 dark fields. We call in a timely way with
only some of them burning.

The small ones cry out & are sent on.

The rounded ones cry out & are sent in.

What shall we say to each other? Let's say, forgive us. We forgive us, we say.

What shall we say to the young poets?

Let's tell them we don't know anything. Let's meet when we are safe
                    with the size of those who sigh.
Let's meet with all our skin tones, glowing . . .

The angels in the back of our eye are safe in their pre-existence.

They come through with as much change as they can manage.

Friends keep saying the system the system,
Amazon trucks with their toxic Prime profits,

devil wind spools over the high basin, wide vortex
over the Atlantic, former glaciers as

everyone's phones eat particles of rotting planet.

We were led out of danger. It was asymmetrical. In sleep, a keel in the back
                    of each blade sent out balancing as now.

There will again be great cities. We escaped in circles as we waited
in a few syllables
in the nothings past the nothings in a few minutes before later—

Epithalamium for Anxiety & Energy

They lived behind the dazzle
of the didn't & fate's blind eye
looked out for them.   For some moments
they were able to relax,
given the no rain. At times everything seemed married.
Maybe it was adjusting
to the massive beauty, not being
brought to some healed place: anxiety & energy
a slight turn to the left, & there
language happened. This love let
centuries recover from violence not silence.

Just because it's a metaphor doesn't
mean it didn't happen,
& if there's no angel, there is one wing to take you

through the color & if there's no
wing there are folds to be assembled—
sparrow with gold heads eating
stale seed like St. Francis might have had.
They had made
outside their solitude vast vowels
in time for grasses to rise
upon the varied worlds, as they do now—

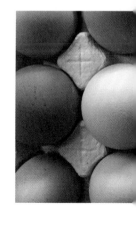

On Hearing the Golden-crowned Sparrow

Half- sweet   squeal.
Sounds like one hearing aid placed on the table . . .

A song knows
more than one way.

      When hills catch fire,
this sparrow stays
(or, returns
      to the same bush   each year—)

                        We loved each other
          when we couldn't love ourselves,

our life a time-shaped miracle.

      A new ash is covering the plants,

planet . . .   plans::

the song's enchantment   has a grainy hunger,

finishingly,   seep-seep,   nightly
finishing   unearthbound,   like a Saturday.
Its broad eyebrows   crowd its crown.

When we are sad about poetry,

            when the immortals can't
be heard   because of fire

            this staggered sound.   Split
splendor   (about

            our height, from the ground—)

Acknowledgments

Deep gratitude as always to Suzanna Tamminen & to the staff at Wesleyan University Press, to Jim Schley, & to Jeff Clark for design. I'm immeasurably indebted to Forrest Gander & to Geoffrey G. O'Brien for early readings of this book in manuscript. Grateful acknowledgment to editors & staff of the following anthologies, magazines, organizations, & venues where these poems appeared, sometimes in collaborative or video forms or in other versions: *About Place Journal*; *Academy of American Poets Poem-a-Day & Dear Poet*; *Alta*; *AWP Writers Chronicle*; *Best American Poetry 2022*; *Bomb Cyclone*; *California Poetry, Volume I* (from Nomadic Coffee); Cap and Bells Press (broadside); *Cascadian Zen* (anthology); The Center for the Book (broadside); *Clade Song*; Climate Change at Glasgow (pamphlet of Jonathan Skinner); *Concision Poetry Journal*; *The Distance Plan 5*; *Echo: a collection of ecopoetical works*; *Ello, The Creators Network* (ellopoetry); *Emergence Magazine*; Empyrean Press (broadside); *The Experiment Will Not Be Bound* (anthology); *Extraction Art*; *Fire & Rain: The Ecopoetry of California* (anthology); *Fractured Ecologies* (anthology); *FUTURE ANTERIOR: COP(oetry) 26*; *Harper's Magazine*; *Harlequin Creature*; Hit & Run Press (broadside); *The Inner Forest Service*; *Interim*; *Interlitq's Californian Poets, Part 4*; *In the American Grain* (anthology); *The Iowa Review*; *The Jung Journal*; *Kenyon Review*; *Lana Turner*; *Lightning Strikes* (anthology); listening-to-gaia.net; *Los Angeles Review of Books*; *Michigan Quarterly Review*; *Mockingbird*; *The New Yorker*; *The New York Times Magazine*; *Orion*; *Pangyrus: The Resistance Issue*; *Harriet* (The Poetry Foundation blog); *Plant-Human Quarterly*; *Ploughshares*; *PoetryNow*; the Poetry Foundation (poetryfoundation.org); The Poetry Project in New York; *Rosebud*; *The Scheherazade Project* (thescheherazadeproject.org); *The Slowdown*; Sonoma County Art Museum ("From Fire, Low Rises" installation); *Stay Inspired* (The Dolby Chadwick Gallery); *Studio One Reading Series: 10 Years: 54 Poets*; *Tin House*; *Together in a Sudden Strangeness*; *Tree Lines: An Anthology of 21st-Century American Poems*; *Volt*; *What Nature*; *World Literature Today*; and *Written Here: The Community of Writers Poetry Review*. The Academy of American Poets partnered with the New York Philharmonic to produce Project 19 (https://poets.org/project-19), celebrating women artists. Thank you to Marjorie Welish for the visionary collaboration & to poet-translators & scholars whose work across disciplines, languages, and materials helped this writing, including Rachel Tzvia Back, Hans Jürgen Balmes, Dan Beachy-Quick, Biwei Yang, Chen Li, John Cha, Don Mee Choi, Norma Cole, CAConrad, Francesca Cricelli, Adam Dickinson, Julia Fiedorczuk, María Gómez de León, Judy

Halebsky, Jack Jung, Claudia Keelan, Lynn Keller, Sebastião Edson Macedo, Nuno Marques, Christopher Merrill, Aaron Moe, "The Poets of No Name" (Burma/Myanmar), Eugene Ostashevsky, Joanna Piechura, Margaret Ronda, Chris Stroffolino, Cole Swensen, Ayako Takahashi, Jami Proctor Xu, Ezequiel Zaidenwerg, & Zhou Zan. Thank you to the following communities for sustaining company: the Academy of American Poets Chancellors & staff; the American Academy of Arts & Sciences; the Community of Writers poets & staff; coven51; the flute girls Reading Group (CS, DG, DL, DN, ER, GC, LM, & PD); the Interfaith Vigil; the Napa Valley Writer's Conference poets & staff; the MFA Program at Saint Mary's College (Matthew Zapruder, thank you for sanity); *Poetry Flash* & Watershed; Prophets Not Profits environmental activist group; Rincon High School Reunion; St. Columba's in Inverness (Jane P's word is "episcopagan"); Eleni Sikelianos's & Marcella Durand's environmental collective; & the Unicorns (AG, AL, AR, DH, DJ, MJ, MZ, RA, SH, VC). Thank you to University of Virginia Creative Writing Program faculty, staff, & students for the opportunity to serve as Kapnick Writer-in-Residence in 2021. These groups offered wonder & pleasure during this struggling time & often encouraged difficult conversations. i have a lot to learn, & my education is ongoing.

To all our children & partners & to our grandchildren: your abiding love sustains us immeasurably; we treasure you each. Deep gratitude to neighbors on our street, especially Ray, Tina, Aaron, Ray, Carolyn, Dan, Lee Lee, & Meryl for food, masks, & company. Sonya Baehr, Eliã Baretto, Nancy Lea Bratt, Susan Briante, Ama Codjoe, Mark Conway, Christina Creveling, Camille Dungy, Elizabeth Farnsworth, Louise Glück, Valyntina Grenier, Marie Howe, Paul Hudelson, Angie Hume, Sarah Karlinsky, Fran Lerner, Karen McClung, Donna Masini, Jane Miller, Jesse Nathan, Nan Norene, Cynthia Parker-Ohene, Sharon Olds, Donald Revell, Amatus Sami-Karim, Nicole Sealey, giovanni singleton, Brian Teare, Jane Vandenburgh, and Hannah Zeavin, thank you. Deep gratitude to Dr. Leif Hass & all the staff at Sutter East Bay Hospital, especially the cardiac team, for your care. Thank you most of all to Bob Hass's heart.

Notes

The writing in this book took place in several geographical spots, mainly on ancestral & unceded lands of the Chochenyo Ohlone, Miwok & Washoe peoples. i acknowledge with respect their Indigenous sovereignty.

—The quote from Rukeyser is taken from "Craft Interview with Muriel Rukeyser" (Cornelia Davis and Mary Jane Fortunato, *New York Quarterly*, 1972).

—"Notes at the West County Detention Center": Before the pandemic, Bob and i took part in a vigil at the facility in Richmond to protest the detention of undocumented persons in a facility; the Sheriff of Contra Costa County moved the detainees to a facility out of the Bay Area that would be less accessible to protestors & families of those being held.

—"Among Some Anapests at Civic Center" refers to a line by Tobias Meneley, "subject to history's impress" in *The Animal Claim: Sensibility and the Creaturely Voice*.

—In the "1967" sequence **ll** refers to footsteps in Berkeley.

—"In Some Senses of the Word" intentionally reverses two letters in "edge."

—"History of Punctuation on the Face" features lines from my own face & that of Nan Norene—gratitude for her beauty.

—"A Child Finishing Fourth Grade Online" quotes Leon Légère with his permission.

—"The Scattering of the Lyric I": Many will know that James Joyce wrote the phrase "silence, exile and cunning," not me, but just in case it needs a note . . .

—"Dear emerging, pre-emerging & post-emerging poets" refers to a blog by writer Lisa Wells.

—"The Sickness & the World Soul" owes a debt to a June 2020 lecture series on apocalypse; thank you to Father Vincent Pizzuto for those talks. The writings of Pat Gilbert, Ron Kagan, & David Robson helped the composition of this sequence; :::[a ragged white moth passes by]::: includes a line by David Robson. The breath drawings were done in a ritual on my iPad.

—"Punctuation at the end of time" refers to Lyn Hejinian's seminal essay "Against Closure."

Debts are also owed for readings in *Pause and Effect: Punctuation in the West* by M. B. Parkes, *Mosses* by Robin Wall Kimmerer, *The Illustrated Glossary of Botanical Terms* by Tony Foster, & the *Laws Field Guide to the Sierra Nevada* by John Muir Laws.

Brenda Hillman is a writer, teacher, editor, and activist. She has published ten collections of poetry from Wesleyan University Press, including *Bright Existence,* a finalist for the Pulitzer Prize, and *Practical Water,* which won the *Los Angeles Times* Book Award for Poetry. With Patricia Dienstfrey, she edited *The Grand Permission: New Writings on Poetics and Motherhood,* and with Helen Hillman, she translated *At Your Feet* by Ana Cristina Cesar. A Chancellor Emerita of the Academy of American Poets, Hillman serves on the faculty of Saint Mary's College in Moraga, California and as a staff poet at Community of Writers and at Napa Valley Writers' Conference. She is married to poet Robert Hass.